The Stranger by Albert Camus

A Critical Introduction

By

Ray Moore M.A.

Dedication:

To Barbara who made everything possible.

Contents

Preface

> In our society, every man who does not cry at his mother's funeral runs the risk of receiving the death penalty ... the hero of the book is given the death sentence because he doesn't play the game. (Camus, Preface to the 1955 U.S. edition of *The Stranger*).

In his "Translator's Note" to the Vintage International Edition of *The Stranger*, Matthew Ward points to the paradoxical nature of this novel: a "profoundly popular" style (which makes the novel a quick and easy read) masks a complex, poetic work in which everything "Meursault says or feels or does resonates with all he does not say, all he does not feel, all he does not do" (*v*). The result is a novel accessible on a first reading which rewards each subsequent re-reading with new insights. Ward makes the further point that as translator his aim is "to capture what he [Camus] said, not what he meant. In theory, the latter should take care of itself" (*vi*). That little phrase, "In theory" is the entire justification for this book.

Some critics conclude that, either by design or because of flaws in the novel, what Camus "meant" in *The Stranger* cannot be explained, that the novel is not capable of a consistent reading. Olivier Todd writes that both Meursault himself and the "deeper meaning" of the novel are "finally inexplicable" (147). The present study is an attempt to refute such assertions.

The popularity of *The Stranger* rests on the fact that since its publication it has continued to capture readers' sense of personal alienation from the forces in society which seek to impose order and conformity. Patrick McCarthy writes that "*The Stranger's* importance ... lies in the way that the novel has caught fundamental traits of modern individualism: the determination to trust one's own experience while distrusting the many and the varied forms of authority" (103). This is one of the reasons why teenagers instinctively feel that they 'get' Meursault. However, there is a danger in the apparent simplicity of the novel, and in its continuing relevance to a multi-generational distrust of authority, that the precise meaning of the work (the meaning which Camus intended it to have) will be lost.

I have taught *The Stranger* for six years, and each time I have taught it, I have deepened my understanding of what Camus "meant": sometimes it has been my own re-reading which has produced a new understanding, but more often it has been a student's contribution to class discussion or a comment in a student's essay. The present book presents to the serious reader and the student alike a coherent reading of the text based on my current understanding of it. I have enough respect for my readers to assume that they will take what they find convincing and reject what they find unconvincing. My aim is to stimulate the reader to develop his/her own understanding of a novel which (and again I speak from classroom experience) profoundly touches the lives of those who make the effort to understand it.

As far as possible, I have tried to make the starting point of my analysis the text itself using the translation by Matthew Ward because it is "the standard reference text of the novel in English" and is the version that most English-speaking readers will use (Gay-Crosier 129). Rather than attempting to place the novel in its historical, cultural, literary, philosophical or biographical contexts in separate chapters, I have integrated these elements into the analysis whenever they seem to shed light on the meaning of the text. Camus rejected the label philosopher; indeed, Professor Poirier annotated Camus' *diplôme d'études supérieures* dissertation with the comment that his student was, "'More a writer than a philosopher'" (quoted in Lottman 109), and Jean-Paul Sartre later maintained that Camus lacked the breadth of reading necessary to understand existentialism. Nevertheless, Camus did claim to be a philosophical novelist. In this study, I have identified in the Introduction the ideas which are central to an understanding of *The Stranger*. This chapter is written for the general reader not for the philosophy student. Although I could not avoid the use of the term the absurd, I have deliberately kept to a minimum references to existentialism since Camus always maintained that he was not an existentialist.

The critical approach which I have adopted is to give a detailed analysis of each chapter, and only then to provide materials which allow the reader to place *The Stranger* in the context of Camus' thought and writing. After studying the text, the reader will develop a deeper understanding of the novel through a combination of further research and re-reading. I have included a brief analysis of his novel *A Happy Death*, which may be regarded as a first draft of *The Stranger* and an account of his philosophical essay *The Myth of Sisyphus* which aims to make this work accessible to the general reader.

Introduction

> A novel is never anything but a philosophy put into images. And in a good novel, all the philosophy has gone into the images. (Camus' review of *Nausea* by Jean-Paul Sartre)

In *The Stranger,* Albert Camus seeks to answer a very precise and limited question: What is the nature of the relationship between man and the world in which man lives out his life?

This might seem to be a dauntingly difficult question until we realize that there are fundamentally only three possible answers. The world may be either: benevolent, malevolent or indifferent – there are no other answers. Despite the fact that each of these three words is normally used to describe human motivation, no one is suggesting that the world is 'alive' or that it has consciousness. Adherents of the benevolent world position believe that the world has a nature which humans can come to understand; we can then use this understanding to act purposefully to improve our lives and in so doing can attain both happiness and success. Rhonda Byrne writes, "The earth turns on its orbit for You. The oceans ebb and flow for You. The sun rises and it sets for You ... You are the master of the Universe" (183). Other examples of this approach to living may be found in Ayn Rand's Benevolent Universe Premise, and in the allegorical novel *The Alchemist* by Paulo Coelho. However, at this point, the 'New Age' benevolent world philosophy disappears from our analysis because, for a combination of historical and intellectual reasons, it is never a viable world view for Camus.

Adherents of the malevolent world position believe that the material world is actually inimical to man who is, by his very nature, helpless and doomed; success, happiness, achievement are impossible or are, at best, the temporary result of pure chance. Traditional Christian theology holds that, as a consequence of the sin of Adam and Eve, for which man was excluded from Paradise, we are fallen creatures living in a corrupt world. The American Puritan theologian and philosopher Jonathan Edwards expresses this view of life in sermons such as "Sinners in the Hands of an Angry God": "Were it not that so is the sovereign Pleasure of God, the Earth would not bear you one Moment; for you are a Burden to it; the Creation groans with you; the Creation is made Subject to the Bondage of your Corruption, not willingly; the Sun don't willingly shine upon you to give you Light to serve Sin and Satan; the Earth don't willingly yield her Increase to satisfy your Lusts." Greek tragedy is based on a similar assumption concerning man's powerlessness in contrast to the gods.

The two viewpoints reviewed thus far argue either that we are fundamentally at home in the world or that we are fundamentally at war with the world, but adherents of the third position hold that the natural world and the universe beyond are alike indifferent to man and to human destiny. Unlike the first two viewpoints which imply religious (or at least a spiritual) belief, the third is essentially humanistic rejecting equally cosmic karma and divine providence.

To return to Camus' question, three dates will indicate a fundamental change in Western thought. In 1654, James Ussher, the Archbishop of Armagh and Primate of All Ireland, dated Creation precisely to the night preceding Sunday, October 23rd, 4004 BC. In 1867, Matthew Arnold published *New Poems* which included "Dover Beach" the third stanza of which reflects the narrator's sense of society's disillusion with religious faith:

> The Sea of Faith
> Was once, too, at the full, and round earth's shore
> Lay like the folds of a bright girdle furled.
> But now I only hear
> Its melancholy, long, withdrawing roar,
> Retreating, to the breath
> Of the night-wind, down the vast edges drear
> And naked shingles of the world.

In 1920, F. Scott Fitzgerald concluded his novel *This Side of Paradise* by describing his protagonist, Amory Blaine, as part of "a new generation … grown up to find all Gods dead, all wars fought, all faiths in man shaken."

The three examples selected are frankly arbitrary and could equally be exchanged for any number of others all tending to show the decline of historical Christianity, by which is meant faith based on the historical authenticity of the Bible. The certitude of Bishop Ussher becomes incompatible with the geological record, resulting in a crisis of faith: loss of faith implies the absence of transcendental solace. If, as Nietzsche asserts in *The Gay Science* (1882), "God is dead" then the values associated with God are merely artificial human constructs. The Ten Commandments, for example, are no more than graffiti on stone, an idea which, depending on one's point of view, might be regarded either as blasphemy or as liberation. Now, *The Stranger* is set firmly in Fitzgerald's world, a post-Judeo-Christian world in which eternal values have been shown not only to have no validity but to have been a childish delusion precisely because God has ceased to be believable.

How does this abstract thinking apply to real life? The spring of 2011 saw a succession of tornadoes (estimated at 1,475) hit the South and Midwest of the U.S.A. causing 536 deaths. The worst single incident occurred in the late afternoon of Sunday, May 22nd, 2011, when Joplin, a city of about 50,000 people in southwest Missouri, was hit by a massive tornado that cut a path through the city nearly six miles long killing 154 people. The area impacted by this devastation falls within America's 'Bible Belt' a name which reflects deep faith rooted in socially conservative evangelical Protestantism. No doubt the faith of some people was tested to breaking point by these events, but for most their faith provided a meaning without which such destruction would have been unendurable. The Christian response is exemplified by the following blog post filed by Jody Herrington-Gettys, a volunteer, on Thursday, May 26th, "Today as we arrived in Joplin, I saw an image in the midst of horrible devastation that deeply touched my heart.

There was a church that was completely destroyed, but the cross steeple remained. It reminded me that when everything else crumbles, faith still stands."

Faith satisfies the human desire for life to have a transcendent meaning, but what of those for whom faith is no longer an option? Their dilemma (and Meursault's problem) is defined by David A. Strintzen, "Confronted by suffering in a world without assured and universally accepted moral standards, many people feel demoralized and without direction. It is too painful to watch the slaughter" (7). To this, it is necessary to add that in a world without transcendent values, not only is suffering meaningless, but (perhaps more shockingly) so are pleasure, happiness, and apparently positive concepts such as love, justice and humanity.

Once it is accepted that God is dead, it is not, however, necessary to reference destructive natural disasters to argue that life is absurd; it is sufficient to remember that we are all mortal. Religions promise a solution to the meaninglessness of being born simply to die by offering visions of immortality, but what if we cannot believe in that wonderful place beyond the clouds which, in *Animal Farm* by George Orwell, Moses the Raven calls "Sugarcandy Mountain"? Most of us 'solve' the existential problem posed by our mortality by simply ignoring that mortality; that is, we accept in a vague, theoretical way that at some point in the future the bio-mechanisms that are the essential prerequisites of our consciousness will fail, but for all practical purposes we live our lives as though we are going to live forever.

There was a particular reason why such evasion was not an option for Albert Camus: at the age of seventeen he was diagnosed with tuberculosis, a disease for which there was at that time no cure. Sprintzen explains the impact that this diagnosis had on Camus' life and work, "That confrontation [with the possibility of an early death] left an indelible scar on Camus' psyche and philosophy, giving deep personal meaning to the experience of life's absurdity. He felt his stay on earth to be both a joyous gift to one in tune with the rhythms of nature and the temporary sojourn of an exile" (34). Catherine Brosman goes further, linking Camus' diagnosis with his later development of the concept of the absurd, "To Camus, the absurd meant first of all the disparity between a young consciousness hungry for experience and crying out for meaning, and a body condemned to illness, ultimately to death" (22).

Meursault shares with Camus what might be termed a heightened sense of his own mortality (the novel opens with the death of Meursault's mother), but unlike Camus he assumes, without ever having given it much thought, that the absurdity of life means that ethical conduct is an illusion, that one choice is as good as another, and that human values are meaningless. Robert Zaretsky defines the reader's initial impression of the strangeness of Meursault thus:

> Meursault's life is not unique: many others have lived equally drab lives; many more have known far worse. What makes Meursault's life different is his refusal or inability to hew it into meaningful narrative. The traditional comforting formulas we impose on our life stories are absent here. Instead, life is one damn thing after another. There is no logic, no hierarchy of importance, no effort of synthesis. Like the clatter rising from the street below Meursault's terrace, it signifies nothing (53).

In *The Stranger*, the characters live out their lives in Amory Blaine's world - the absurdity of life is a given.

In form, *The Stranger* is a *bildungsroman*, that is, a novel about the moral and intellectual growth of the (young) main character. Understanding this point will prevent a great deal of misunderstanding. English Showalter Jr. describes Meursault's character in Part One as one in which "apathetic ignorance produces a small monster of pure egotism" (72). As a generalization, this statement is hard to fault, but it is simply not possible to generalize about Meursault's character because his character develops from the first line of the novel. Showalter is more accurate when he states that "*The Stranger* relates a progress toward understanding" (93). The news of his mother's death begins a sequence of events which will pull him out of his comfortable cocoon of disengagement until he is face to face with life's ultimate question. It is true that Meursault only comes fully to understand man's relationship with the world and with his own mortality (the two are essentially the same thing) at the end of the novel. Bespaloff succinctly expresses what it is that Meursault comes to understand, "Amid the indifference of a world devoid of god, nothing has any importance or value, <u>except</u> the pure act of living" (emphasis added 95). At this point, the novel ends without attempting to explore the questions which follow naturally: *How* should human beings respond to this reality? *How* should we live? *What* should we do? Camus, who was deeply concerned with ethical values and with establishing "a valid justification for life," would be fascinated by these questions for the rest of his life (Rhein 33). His search for answers to them would lead to the personal and philosophical rift with existential philosopher Jean Paul Sartre, and to the struggle to find a moral position on Algerian independence. In Meursault's story, however, Camus aims to do no more than to establish a foundation upon which to examine questions which are vitally important to every reader.

PART ONE Chapter 1: A Very Singular Man

> *Rosencrantz:* Did you ever think of yourself as actually dead, lying in a box with a lid on it?
> *Guildenstern:* No.
> *Rosencrantz:* Nor do I, really. It's silly to be depressed by it. I mean, one thinks of it like being alive in a box. One keeps forgetting to take into account the fact that one is dead, which should make all the difference, shouldn't it? (Tom Stoppard, *Rosencrantz and Guildenstern Are Dead*)

Consider the following:

1. Re-read paragraph one. It establishes Meursault as the narrator/protagonist. Comment on Meursault's reaction to the news of the death of his mother:

a) his use of the word informal, colloquial "Maman" (very roughly 'mom' rather than 'mother' which would be 'ma mere');

b) the aspects of her death that do concern him;

c) anything that you find lacking in his response;

d) possible meanings (including those that the narrator may not intend) of his statement, "That doesn't mean anything" (3). [You should find three or four.];

e) the writer's use of short sentences to reflect the narrator's reaction.

2. Meursault concentrates throughout the chapter on practical details. These seem to interest him whereas social relationships seem to bore and even antagonize him. Give examples of some of the practical details that capture his interest.

3. Meursault is often surprised or even irritated by displays of emotion in others. Give examples. What do these have in common? How does this commonality explain his feelings? How does Meursault seek to block out emotion?

4. Comment on the description of Perez falling behind the coffin and finally fainting at the cemetery. Does Camus intend this to be comic? Does it contain a symbolic meaning?

5. In this chapter, Meursault repeatedly feels guilty or embarrassed. Give examples. What do these have in common? How does this commonality help the reader to understand his feelings?

6. Comment on the following dialogue between the nurse and Meursault, "She said, 'If you go slowly, you risk getting sunstroke. But if you go too fast, you work up a sweat and then catch a chill inside the church.' She was right. There was no way out" (17).This appears to be a comment on the power of the heat, but Meursault's conclusion suggests a more symbolic interpretation. Against what does Meursault feel there is "no way out"? [Note: He may or may not be conscious that his words carry this deeper meaning. What do you think?]

7. The chapter ends with Meursault listing a number of "images from that day that have stuck in my mind" (17-18). What do they have in common? What is the sole image that generates an emotional response in Meursault?

8. How do you react to Meursault's apparent lack of emotion about his mother's death? Is his indifference a sign of honesty or lack of humanity or both?

The Setting of the Novel:

Albert Camus referred in his Nobel Prize speech to the "'more than twenty years of absolutely insane history,' when he felt 'lost hopelessly like all those of [his] age in the convulsions of the epoch'" (quoted in Brée *Albert Camus* 9).

Perhaps it was this very sense of being lost in the vast political changes of a particularly traumatic epoch which led Camus essentially to write history out of *The Stranger*.

The protagonist of *The Stranger* is Meursault (no first name is ever given), a shipping clerk in his mid-twenties who works for a firm in Algiers. Like Camus, Meursault is a *pied-noir*, a French citizen, nominally Catholic, born in Algeria to the descendents of French colonists. Raymond Gay-Crosier points out that in *A Happy Death* the protagonist is called Patrice Mersault, a name which is "a combination of *mer* (sea) and *soleil* (sun)" (10). The minor change in spelling to Meursault in *The Stranger* appears not to invalidate this identification; the protagonist's name thus suggests both the Mediterranean life-style of the *pied-noir* in general and Meursault's particular tendency to experience life almost exclusively through his five senses.

Although the novel was written in the years leading up to the outbreak of World War Two and was published in 1942 in German-occupied France, it makes no reference to the War. Similarly, despite the fact that during late 1930s and early 1940s Arab nationalism was a growing force in Algeria, the narrative contains no specific reference to political tensions which would result in the outbreak of the Algerian Revolution in 1954 leading to the declaration of Algerian Independence on July 5, 1962, which effectively marked the end French colonialism. The novel, then, is set in a pre-War Algeria, one clearly based on Camus' memory of the Algeria of his childhood and youth, in which the wider political and social questions of the mid-twentieth century do not intrude into the individual lives which the novel chronicles. Showalter writes that "the setting is almost incidental. The character [Meursault] could be almost any nationality, the time could be almost any year in the twentieth century, the place could be almost any large city with a beach and a hot climate" (2).

The Algeria in the narrative has an "aura of timelessness" (Gay-Crosier 38) and is, in this sense, ahistorical: it provides a quasi-realistic setting which Camus exploits to present the timeless questions of human existence uncomplicated by the socio-political crises which dominated the times in which the novel was written. This is enough to alert the reader to the fact that, despite its apparent realism in describing characters and events, the novel does not fall conveniently into the genre realism. Rachel Bespaloff argues that Camus consciously adopts a "realism which I shall call 'cryptic,' to distinguish it from naturalistic realism" (92). Beynon John makes a similar point when he comments that, *"The Stranger*, far from being a transcript of the real world, is an allegory, a veritable myth of the absurd as incarnated in Meursault" (88). Similarly, Showalter writes that the novel is "something more like a parable" than a realistic presentation of Meursault's experience (94).

Meursault as Narrator:

At a 1957 press conference in Stockholm shortly before he received the Nobel Prize for Literature, Herbert Lottman reports Camus as saying that, "Of his fictional characters, he could not identify any one of them as his spokesman" (615). This parallels what Camus wrote in the same year, "A character is never the novelist who created him" (quoted in Brosman 123). Bearing these statements in mind will prevent a great deal of misunderstanding of what Camus is actually saying in this novel.

Meursault's story, and the story of his intellectual and emotional development, is told in the first-person, a technique which tends to make the reader empathize with the narrator. This form of narrative, however, causes the reader some problems of interpretation in *The Stranger*. Are we to assume that the novel is a written journal, and, if so, at what points were its different sections written? In his study of the novel, Patrick McCarthy attempts to divide the narrative into sections and to indicate when they could have been written, but in doing so he repeatedly draws attention to what he regards as deliberate flaws in the novel's chronology from which he concludes that, as part of his intended criticism of the French journal-novel, "Camus does not wish to present a temporal structure that is clear" (25). A simpler alternative is to conclude that the concept of the narrative-as-journal is not helpful in understanding this novel. There are, in fact, no indications in the narrative that Camus intends it to be read as a journal (no dated entries, no references to the act of writing, etc.); indeed, Meursault, a man who for most of the novel takes pride in asserting that he has "pretty much lost the habit of analyzing myself," is the last person one would expect to keep a journal (65).

The attempt to find a realistic context (or frame-story) for the narrative which we read is as ultimately unrewarding as is the attempt to place the action in the real pre-War Algiers. Meursault is telling us the story, or rather Meursault is telling the story to himself and we eavesdrop since the reader is given no identity or independent reality; that is to say, the novel is an interior monologue rather than a dramatic monologue, what Showalter describes as "a silent meditation addressed to no one" (67). Neither is it profitable to divide the narrative into sections each written at different times. It makes much more sense of the narrative to conclude that Meursault relates his whole story at some point between the end of the novel and his execution so that everything is told in retrospect. John Fletcher similarly concludes that "the account is written with the benefit of considerable hindsight ... [The reader] establishes that the book, which at the outset appear to be a diary, is in fact *entirely* composed ... in the days (or hours) which follow the rejection of the prisoner's appeal and the consequential certitude it brings that the time he has left is finite" (quoted in Bloom ed. 68-9, original emphasis).

This interpretation explains why there is only an apparent contradiction between Meursault, the unreflective character in Part One, and Meursault the reflective narrator, though two important caveats need to be noted. Firstly, as we shall see, the opening two paragraphs of the novel are written in the present tense; indeed, Meursault even uses the future tense to describe actions which he plans to take, "I'll take the two o'clock bus" before transferring to the past tense at the start of paragraph three, "I caught the two o'clock bus" (3). This does not mean that these paragraphs were *written* immediately after Meursault received the telegram announcing his mother's death (a most unlikely reaction!) or that there is a gap in time between Meursault narrating paragraphs two and three. In fact, there is no great mystery or difficulty here: Meursault begins his narrative by recapturing, in real time, the incident which first disrupted his life; he is re-living moments so intense that they will always be *now* for him. Or, say that Camus felt it to be essential that the reader should experience these moments literally alongside Meursault in the present. It amounts to the same thing: we are looking at a question of style here (whether we choose to regard it as Meursault's or Camus' style) and not of chronology.

The second point is more fundamental. Although Meursault does not begin to tell his story until after he has understood its full significance, he makes every effort in the narrative not to interpret past actions on the basis of this future knowledge. Camus ensures that Meursault explains every incident in terms of what he felt and understood at the time precisely because what he felt and understood at the time was so often entirely wrong (as he only now understands). To the author, this limited perspective is essential to his aim that the reader should grow to understanding *with* Meursault and not just have Meursault's growth explained *by* an omniscient narrator.

Only very occasionally does Meursault interpose a judgment which depends upon his later understanding. This happens much less than some critics have supposed. For example, when he hears from the director of the home that his mother requested a religious funeral, Meursault tells us that he is surprised commenting, "While not an atheist, Maman had never in her life given a thought to religion" (6). McCarthy feels that at this point Meursault inconsistently "slips into the role of the omniscient author," but this is not true (26). Meursault is making a perfectly reasonable assertion based on having grown up for over two decades with his mother - perfectly reasonable, and, as the novel later reveals, completely incorrect, for Maman *did* think about religion towards the end of her life, something which Meursault comes to understand only at the end of his story. On those few occasions when Meursault wishes to draw attention to the difference between how he felt at the time and how he feels now, he makes it perfectly clear that this is what he is doing. For example, when he watches the old people at Maman's vigil, he is so unsympathetic to them that he cannot believe that what they are doing is meaningful even to themselves simply because it is not meaningful to him, a judgment which he will finally understand to be erroneous, "I even had the impression that the dead woman lying in front of them didn't mean anything to them. But I think now that this was a false impression" (emphasis added 11). In many ways, this statement is a microcosm of the novel: Meursault the protagonist is a man who is unaware, who sleep-walks through life, and we accompany him, only learning the significance of what he (and through him we) experienced at the end of the narrative - a few hours before everything is wiped out.

One of the Most Famous Openings in the Twentieth Century Novel:

The novel begins with Meursault's stark statement, "Maman died today" (3). Since such a memorable opening is likely to have a significant impact on the reader's attitude towards Meursault, it is important to pause in order to consider two challenges posed by the sentence as Camus originally wrote it, "Aujourd'hui, Maman est morte." The first problem is how to render the word "Maman" for the English or American reader since it has no exact equivalent. Stuart Gilbert, Camus' first translator (in 1946), opted for the word 'mother' in which decision he was followed by the translations of both Joseph Laredo and Kate Griffith (1982). Ryan Bloom criticizes this rendering arguing, "There is little warmth, little bond or closeness or love in 'Mother,' which is a static, archetypal term, not the sort of thing we use for a living, breathing being with whom we have close relations." This word-choice certainly makes Meursault appear distant and cold-hearted which does not appear to be Camus' intention. (Without wishing to press the point too far and so to fall into the simplistic view that Camus is writing autobiography rather than fiction, Camus, despite Madame Camus' profound deafness and her illiteracy which tended to inhibit their communication, had tremendous regard and affection for his own mother, who was very much alive at the time he wrote *The Stranger*.) No translator has opted for the apparently obvious words 'mum,' 'mummy,' 'mom,' or 'mommy' probably because, although these may be linguistically equivalent, they are not culturally equivalent: no adult in either England or America would use any of them because they are more appropriate to children. Thus, Matthew Ward opts to retain the French word "Maman" and in doing so ensures that the reader's first impression (which will be borne out by the novel) is that Meursault does have affectionate memories of his mother; he just does not love her in the way in which society requires of him.

The second problem posed by this opening statement is that the French language naturally places the adverb 'today' at the start of the sentence whilst English syntax naturally places it at the end, which is where all translators have put it. This is unfortunate since Camus' sentence as written carries an important implication about the way in which Meursault perceives events: to him events occur chronologically but in isolation. Meursault lives in the moment, his perception of the world being more like a succession of still photographs than a movie because he does not connect events either emotionally or causally. As R.W.B. Lewis points out, "Meursault's favorite conjunction is the colorless 'and' – never 'since,' 'because,' or 'therefore'" (quoted in Bloom ed. 57). Thus, although the unanimous decision of translators is understandable (even correct), it nevertheless robs the reader of an important indication of Meursault's view of his relationship to the world which is, after all, the central concern of the novel.

Two Languages in Collision:

Meursault's reaction to the news of the death of his mother is presented by Camus as an interior monologue in the present tense. His thoughts, captured in real-time, are expressed in short, disjointed sentences which suggest his inability to respond coherently to the news he has just received. His language is personal, tentative, and inconclusive, very different (as we shall see) from that of the telegram. The contrast between Meursault's choice of the familiar term "Maman" and the word "Mother" which is used in the formal and emotionless language of the telegram suggests, as has been argued, some closeness to and tenderness towards his mother, but what the reader finds shocking is that, this being so, Meursault exhibits no grief over her death. He appears, rather, to fixate on the intellectual problem of establishing a time of death as an alternative to, an evasion of, the expression of sorrow for the loss of someone for whom he might have been expected to feel love.

The mathematical problem which appears to fascinate Meursault is whether his mother died on the day that the telegram was sent or on the day before it was sent. Finally, Meursault decides that the data presented in the telegram is insufficient for him to decide the issue, "'Mother deceased. Funeral tomorrow. Faithfully yours.' That doesn't mean anything. Maybe it was yesterday" (3). On the conscious level, Meursault's comment, "That doesn't mean anything" relates to the inconclusive nature of the telegram which offers no evidence by which definitively to date his mother's death: Did she die the day the telegraph was sent or the day before? There are, however, two other interpretations of Meursault's dismissive comment which, although the narrator seems not to be aware of them, become significant to the reader later in the novel. Firstly, it could be the standard valediction (or complimentary close) "Faithfully yours" which is felt to be meaningless because it is merely conventional and thus patently insincere: the writer means nothing by it for the simple reason that he barely knows the person to whom he is writing.

It is placed there in conformity to social convention: it is a meaningless gesture. Secondly, it could be the death of his mother itself which is meaningless to Meursault: it means nothing because her death was something that was always going to happen, and, this being so, it does not touch Meursault, and he does not grieve. The reader is at this stage in the novel likely to attribute Meursault's lack of emotional reaction to the news of his mother's death to shock: he has not yet begun to grieve. Such an interpretation is based on the assumption that Meursault's psychology is 'normal'. However, it soon becomes clear that Meursault is constitutionally incapable of spontaneously feeling emotions, a failing which society will find to be both abnormal and abhorrent.

Up to this point, our analysis of the opening of the novel has followed conventional lines: critics have focused on Meursault's reaction to the telegram. Less emphasis has been given to analyzing the language of the telegram itself, although Patrick McCarthy draws our attention to the fact that in reading the telegram Meursault has the first of many encounters with "the language of authority" (16). The telegram is an official communication from a state-run institution, and it utilizes the same language which is used by Meursault's boss, the director of the old peoples' home, and by the state judicial system The message is brief, authoritative, purely formal, and anonymous, "'Mother deceased. Funeral tomorrow. Faithfully yours,'" and as such it stands in complete contrast to the uncertain, hesitant and confused nature of Meursault's reaction to it (3). If critics are so willing to find Meursault's reaction to the telegram odd, unusual, even abnormal, should we not apply the same criteria to the telegram itself? When we do, we are forced to conclude that as a piece of communication it is brutally unfeeling and efficiently utilitarian. Whilst telegrams tend to be brief, the writer has not found the time, the care, or the money for a single sympathetic word – not one! McCarthy points out that the director's use of the euphemism "deceased" (which he translates as "passed away") can be contrasted with Meursault's blunter and more honest statement that his mother "died" (3). The inhuman nature of the first four words of the telegram makes the final two words simply insulting. How dare the writer claim to be faithful to the recipient?

This is the language of authority, of society. The purpose of the telegram is to normalize death, to contain it by making it official, to depersonalize and dehumanize it – ultimately, by the use of euphemism, to deny it. This point is vitally important, for Meursault will later claim (both implicitly and explicitly) that society is fooling itself with its apparent reverence for values such as love and justice. The telegram is the first piece of evidence which Camus gives the reader which tends to validate Meursault's point that he has the same feelings (or rather the same lack of feelings) as everyone else, and that the only difference between him and everybody else is that he is more honest about it than are they. Thus a comparison between the language which the telegram uses to announce Maman's death and the language which Meursault uses to come to terms with the news clearly influences the reader to be more sympathetic to Meursault.

Meursault's Reaction to His Mother's Death:

Commentators frequently use the word "indifferent" to describe Meursault's reaction to the news of his mother's death. (Spark Notes uses the word three times in the first paragraph of its "Analysis of Chapter One".) It is a convenient term to use because the same word will be used by Camus right at the end of the novel to describe Meursault's final understanding of his relationship with the world, "I opened myself to the gentle indifference of the world" (122). However, it is important to note that the word is not used in Chapter One. In fact, the use of this term involves two fundamental errors of interpretation. Firstly, in claiming that he reacts with indifference to the news of his mother's death, critics are applying to Meursault the same erroneous judgment that society applies throughout the novel. It is true that Meursault does not show conventional signs of grief for the death of a loved one; indeed, he does not feel grief. However, to assume that this means that his reaction is indifference is to believe, as the society in this novel clearly does believe, that there are only two choices for Meursault: to feel and to express conventional grief for his mother or to be "'morally guilty of killing his mother'" (101-2). These are not the only possible reactions. Secondly, and even more importantly, labeling Meursault's reaction to his mother's death "indifferent" (remember that Camus does not use this word) implies that Meursault feels about his mother's death when he *first* hears of it exactly as he feels about it after his epiphany at the end of the narrative, and this is simply not true. Such an interpretation ignores the fact that the whole point of the novel is to illustrate Meursault's changing understanding of the relationship of life and death: indifference is a state which Meursault *must achieve*, not one in which he is already living at the start of the narrative.

The truth is much more complex and much more interesting, for, in fact, Meursault does not react as though his mother's death "does not matter one way or the other ... [is] of no importance or value one way or the other ... [elicits] no special liking for or dislike" ("indifferent" defined by Miriam-Webster). Actually, Meursault has a number of reactions to the death of his mother. One which does him no credit is irritation because the death places upon him an obligation to attend the funeral which will force him to interrupt his schedule, and to do this he will first have to go through an unpleasant interview with his boss in which he will use the word "excuse" to justify his request for two days off work (3). Irritation is not admirable, but it is not indifference either.

A second reaction is what Meursault himself will later call love - *not* love as it is defined by society but as it is understood by Meursault. Recall that he has seldom seen his mother since she entered the old-peoples' home three years previously, and that he had nothing in common with her (except biology) when she lived with him prior to that. Three years ago, when she went into the home, Meursault found the apartment "too big," so he moved the dining room table into his bedroom and began to live in just one room; as a result, her death will have no practical impact on his life (21). It will have no emotional impact because mother and son had ceased to communicate long before she went to the home, "When she was at home with me, Maman used to spend her time following me with her eyes, not saying a thing" (5). Nevertheless, society demands that he should grieve for the loss of someone for whom he clearly feels no sense of loss. This is why critics use the word 'indifferent' to describe Meursault's apparent lack of reaction, but it is still a fundamental misunderstanding of what he actually does feel about his mother's death.

Later in the novel, Meursault's defense counsel will ask him if he can say in court that Meursault held back his "natural feelings" at the funeral of his mother, and he will reply, "'No, because it's not true'" (65), yet during his interrogation, when the magistrate asks Meursault if he "loved Maman," he replies, "'<u>Yes</u>, the same as anyone'" (emphasis added 67). The nature of the love which Meursault claims to have felt for his mother is explained when he tells his defense counsel, "What I can say for certain is that I would rather Maman hadn't died" (65). It is unclear (and ultimately irrelevant) whether Meursault means simply that he regrets her death because it resulted in a great many problems for him, whether he is expressing good-will towards his mother, or whether it is combination of the two. What Meursault says, his lawyer finds totally inadequate because he judges it against society's conception of a grieving son; no honest reader, however, could mistake Meursault's reaction for indifference.

Thus, Meursault is not simply 'indifferent' to his mother's death if that means having no feeling about the event; rather, he instinctively rejects the conventional definition of 'love' because it is a fraud, and because he feels that those who use it are pretending to an emotion which they do not actually feel. Recall that, when he first arrives at the Marengo home, Meursault fully intends to view his mother's dead body, "I wanted to see Maman right away" (4). No indifference there! It is only *after* he has experienced the way in which the institution formalizes the grieving process that he changes his mind; Meursault wants nothing to do with what McCarthy calls this "inauthentic mourning" not because he is indifferent to the death of his mother but because his feelings for her are his own and are not to be made the subject of display (31).

Mourning Man's Mortality:

The opening sentences of the chapter introduce one of the central themes of the novel: man's relationship to time. Man is mortal, and death ends everything. In his philosophical essay *The Myth of Sisyphus*, Camus explains the relationship between mortality and time: since there are no "eternal values," the honest man necessarily "situates himself in relation to time ... He admits that he stands at a certain point on a curve that he acknowledges having to travel to its end. He belongs to time..." (13). Unlike every other character in the novel, Meursault knows this, but he knows it instinctively not intellectually – he is a shipping clerk, not a philosopher or a novelist. Moreover, until his final epiphany, Meursault knows only the horror of this truth, a horror which appears to rob life of any value.

The Flight from Emotion:

Meursault's avoidance of emotion, which is facilitated by his obsession with practical details, continues as he plans his journey to the old people's home at Marengo with almost military precision, "eighty kilometers from Algiers ... take the two o'clock bus ... get there in the afternoon ... come back tomorrow night ... [ask] my boss for two days off" (3). The constant reference to numbers here shows that Meursault is most comfortable when he operates at the level of logistics, a characteristic which, incidentally, makes him very good at his job. Meursault eats lunch "at Celeste's, as usual" (3), the first of many indications of the importance of routine in his life, nor has he forgotten the practical detail of obtaining the socially mandated symbols of mourning: a black tie and arm band. However, the fact that he borrows these from his friend Emmanuel, who "lost his uncle a few months back," is another indication of his lack of personal commitment to the public display of emotion and of his exclusively practical nature (4).

He is prepared to go along with social convention because it is expected of him, but he invests the symbols which society values so highly with no personal significance. They are useful to him only in that, "After the funeral ... the case will be closed, and everything will have a more official feel to it" (3). Meursault's use of metaphor here is revealing. He compares what he is going through to a criminal investigation because, once the police have found and convicted the malefactor, the police close the case and move on to the next investigation. This reflects his own hope that following the "official" funeral his life will return to its previous serenity. This word choice is, however, ironic since later Meursault will be placed on trial effectively because "[police] investigators had learned that [he] had 'shown insensitivity' [on] the day of Maman's funeral" (64). At present, he feels "almost as if Maman weren't dead" because her death is not real to him; however, this clearly makes him uncomfortable because he perceives himself as unable to make it real to his boss (3). Once his mother is buried, Meursault hopes that her death will be officially recognized by everyone and that he will no longer be called upon to display emotions which he does not actually feel. He instinctively wishes to bring to his life the practical and emotionless simplicity of life at the office where each transaction can be shown to have been completed by a date-stamp.

The Protocols of Mourning:

Meursault is immediately defensive when he asks his boss for two days off uncomfortably referring to his reason as "an excuse," a term which suggests both his need to justify taking time off work and his desire to receive his boss's forgiveness for doing so (3). When Meursault records that his boss "wasn't too happy about it," this indicates Meursault's instinctive awareness that his failure to show an emotional reaction is socially unacceptable; it is only the first example of Meursault projecting his inner feelings of guilt onto others who he assumes to be judging him or actually accusing him of behaving in an anti-social way when it is clear to the reader that they are not doing so (3).

If lack of emotion is the first indication of Meursault's difference from the other characters in the novel, the second is the difficulty he has in reading the emotions of others. It is clear to the reader that Meursault misinterprets the look of grave sympathy with which his boss receives the news of his mother's death for the boss being unhappy about having to grant an employee two days' leave. Meursault is immediately apologetic, "I even said, 'It's not my fault.' He didn't say anything. Then I thought I shouldn't have said that. After all, I didn't have anything to apologize for. He's the one who should have offered his condolences. But he probably will day after tomorrow, when he sees I'm in mourning" (3) Aware that he is not reacting in the way that society expects a person who is grieving to react, Meursault is too quick to offer an apology and immediately realizes that he has made another misstep. He takes some comfort in thinking through, in a rather mechanical way, his understanding of social protocol and in doing so finds confidence that the criticism which he (falsely) detects in the boss's reaction will disappear when, following the funeral, his boss sees him wearing the socially approved symbols of mourning (black tie and arm band) which will relieve him of the need to actually express grief.

Aware that he does not feel the emotions which society mandates that he should feel, Meursault does his best to behave in acceptably. Thus, on the one hand, he shows his awareness of the importance of social conventions and of playing by the unwritten rules of society, but, on the other hand, he seems to be a stranger in this social world, unable to play by these rules without conscious deliberation and effort because he has not internalized these conventions and rules.

Meursault is similarly at a loss to react appropriately even to the sympathy which he receives from people at Celeste's who he regards as his friends. Significantly, he introduces this episode by observing, "It was very hot" which is the first of many times that Meursault will associate feelings of social pressure with the discomfort caused by the heat of the Algerian summer – it is a motif throughout the novel (3). He recognizes his friends' expressions of concern, but he does not respond, a failing for which he seeks to excuse himself (significantly *to himself* rather than to them) by claiming to be "a little distracted" by the need to visit Emmanuel before catching the bus (4). Once again, logistical details offer a refuge from reflection and feeling. Meursault clearly regards the ceremonies of mourning dress as a formality; he understands that he is required to satisfy the demands of society by going through the mourning ritual which is to him meaningless, but far from enabling him to return to the life he was living before his mother's death, as he clearly hopes, his failure to play convincingly the role of grieving son will begin a chain of events which will lead to his trial and execution.

Evading Social Interactions:

Camus' description of the bus journey to Marengo introduces two more significant features of Meursault's character. The first is his hyper-sensitive to sense impressions: the "bumpy" ride, the "smell of gasoline," and "the glare of the sky" add to the discomfort that Meursault already feels from having had to run in the heat of the afternoon to catch the bus (4). In response, he falls asleep. It is important to note precisely how Meursault describes this: he says that he sleeps "probably because of" the negative sense impressions (4). That is, sleeping is presented by Meursault as an involuntary action almost as if it were compelled upon him by circumstances, whilst Camus suggests that sleep is actually a defense or evasion mechanism which Meursault unconsciously uses whenever he is placed in an uncomfortable position.

The second characteristic is Meursault's need to evade social interactions which make him feel uncomfortable. He successfully escapes negative physical sensations by sleeping most of the journey; however, when Meursault wakes, a soldier sitting next to him attempts to engage him in a conversation which would necessarily lead him to talk about the reason for his trip and thus the death of his mother. Meursault will later in the novel explain the avoidance mechanism which he consciously uses in such situations, "whenever I want to get rid of someone I'm not really listening to, I made it appear as if I agree with them" (69). In this case, he simply lies in order to avoid talking about things that he does not wish to talk about with a person who he does not wish to talk to, "a soldier... smiled at me and asked if I'd been traveling long. I said, 'Yes,' just so I wouldn't have to say anything else" (4).

It is often erroneously stated that Meursault is the only honest character in the novel because he is the only character who refuses to pretend to have emotions which he does not feel and who makes no attempt to hide his lack of feelings. Not only does this view willfully ignore the many lies which Meursault tells (the letter he writes for Raymond Sintès and the testimony he gives to the police in Sintès' defense are both entirely dishonest), it ignores the reality that, for most of Part One, Meursault does little other than dishonestly pretend to fit into a society in which he feels himself to be an outsider. To keep up his pretense, Meursault is forced both to appear to conform to social conventions which he knows to be meaningless and to give the impression that he has feelings which he knows that he does not have in order to convince others that he is "'the same as anyone'" (66). Showalter points to the example of his interaction with the boss in this chapter as showing "the extent of Meursault's concern about social forms and his readiness to observe the etiquette" (62). In this sense, Meursault is just as dishonest as any other character in the novel and perhaps more culpably dishonest since Meursault is conscious of his use of deception to avoid uncomfortable social situations. It is only in Part Two that, as Camus wrote in a retrospective interpretation of the novel, "[Meursault] doesn't play the game ... refuses to lie ... refuses to disguise his feelings" (quoted in Bloom ed. 78).

What *is* true of Meursault in Part One is firstly that when he is directly challenged to express emotions which he does not feel (professional ambition, love, pity for a woman's suffering) he refuses absolutely to do so, and secondly that Meursault so frequently fails effectively to hide his lack of emotion that his failure to feel will ultimately be interpreted as in implicit challenge to society's moral standards, which dictate that one must grieve over death or sacrifice one's claim to humanity. It is ultimately these characteristics for which he will be placed on trial – for being a stranger.

The Challenge of Social Expectations:

Meursault describes his arrival at the Marengo home in a series of short, simple sentences, "The home was two kilometers from the village. I walked them. I wanted to see Maman right away. But the caretaker told me I had to see the director first. He was busy, so I waited awhile" (4). These disjoined statements illustrate the way that Meursault sees events as happening *to* him rather than as initiated *by* him. Significantly, he also presents himself as the victim of causality, controlled by not controlling events.

The meeting with the director of the home brings Meursault for a second time into confrontation with the language of authority. The man is the first of a series of unnamed characters with whom Meursault will interact, characters whose identities are entirely defined by their roles in society and the state. He also wears "the ribbon of the Legion of Honor" (a decoration that Camus himself refused) which specifically links him to the central government in Paris (4). He refers to Maman as "'Madame Meursault'" and gets his information about her from her "file"; he patronizingly calls Meursault "'my dear boy'" (4). (The chaplain will later insist on calling him "'my son'" despite Meursault's objections [120].) The director's entire aim seems to be to minimize the disruption which Maman's death causes to the running of the home by taking away as much of its emotional impact as possible. He tells Meursault, "'We've moved her to our little mortuary. So as not to upset the others.

Whenever one of the residents dies, the others are a bit on edge for the next two or three days. And that makes it difficult to care for them'" (5). Notice the distinction implicit in this statement between 'we,' the authorities in control, and 'them,' those being controlled. Notice again the use of euphemism, "'moved her ... a bit on edge,'" and the focus of concern being on the convenience of the institution. Bloom comments of the director that, "For him, old people, or perhaps people overall, seem to be too much trouble" (Bloom ed. 22).

As with the earlier account of his meeting with the boss, the exchange with the director illustrates the difficulty Meursault has in reading the intentions of others, "he shook me by the hand and held it so long I didn't know how to get it loose" (4). Meursault does not understand that the length of the handshake is intended as a gesture to convey sympathy and support; to him, it is merely physically discomforting. Aware at some level that his relationship with and feelings for his mother do not match the expectations of society, Meursault is once again defensive and perceives criticism where none is intended, "He thumbed through a file and said, 'Madame Meursault came to us three years ago. You were her sole support.' I thought he was criticizing me for something and I started to explain. But he cut me off. 'You don't have to justify yourself, my dear boy'" (4). Meursault's use of the word "something" is both evasive and dishonest. He knows very well what he might be criticized for, and, since the director goes to great lengths to reassure him that his action was both understandable from his own point of view and in his mother's best interests, one must assume that the criticism comes from *within*: Meursault knows that he placed his mother in the home out of a selfish desire to get her out of his life.

Meursault is painfully aware that he did not love his mother in the way demanded by society, and so he retreats into self-justification. What follows foreshadows the trial at which he will be described as "a man who is morally guilty of killing his mother," but ironically on this occasion Meursault is himself both prosecutor and defender (101-2). Presenting the case for his own defense, Meursault explains away the fact that in her first days at the home his mother "cried a lot" as merely a result of her not being "used to it," because any other explanation would involve acknowledging that she felt abandoned and unloved (5). Further, Meursault attempts to justify his failure to visit his mother on the grounds that he did not want to disturb her tranquility. The truth, however, comes to the surface despite Meursault's attempts at evasion when he cites his purely selfish reasons, "the trouble of getting to the bus, buying tickets, and spending two hour traveling" (5). This list of practical inconveniencies suggests a superficial honesty in acknowledging his own selfishness, but it dishonestly evades the real reason why he did not visit: meeting his mother would have made emotional demands upon him which he knew he would be unable to meet just as continuing to live with her in the apartment had. Putting his mother into the Marengo home was another avoidance strategy, and Meursault knows it.

The next social challenge which Meursault must face is the expectation that a son will naturally want to see his dead mother's body. It is important to remember that, before his encounter with the director, this was precisely what Meursault intended to do, but the director really offers Meursault no opportunity to refuse by making an assumption about Meursault's wishes based upon his expectation of grieving sons, "'I suppose you'd like to see your mother'" (5). Illustrating a feature of his character which will become important in the novel, Meursault at first acquiesces to the suggestion when it is presented by the director, a person of whom he is somewhat in awe (he has just called him "'sir'"), "I got up without saying anything and he led me to the door" (5). The word "led" indicates that Meursault is being guided not by his own will but by the stronger will of the director augmented by the power of his own impulse toward social conformity.

When he enters the room which contains the coffin, Meursault's hyper-sensitivity to sense impressions is again evident. His description of the room, which concentrates on visual impressions of color and texture, reads like a detailed list or inventory, "a very bright, whitewashed room with a skylight ... some chairs and some cross-shaped sawhorses ... a closed casket ... some shiny screws ... an Arab nurse in a white smock, with a brightly colored scarf" (6). Meursault meticulously records the appearance of everything without appearing to understand the significance of anything. For example, he notes that the screws on the coffin are "not skewed down all the way, [but are] standing out against the walnut-stained planks" without drawing the obvious conclusion that they have been left this way in order to make his viewing of the body easier. It is left to the caretaker to explain this. Tellingly, Meursault's first mention of the coffin uses the indefinite article 'a' because to use the definite article 'the' would be to recognize the significance of this particular coffin. What is excluded from Meursault's description is any recognition that the coffin contains his mother's body.

Without being overtly conscious of it, Meursault is here being exposed to society's attempt to institutionalize death, and (partly because of this, and perhaps because he is now accompanied by the caretaker rather than the director) Meursault summons the courage to assert his will to resist the pressures of expectation, although he immediately feels that he has made a social blunder, "He was moving towards the casket when I stopped him. He said, 'You don't want to?' I answered, 'No.' He was quiet, and I was embarrassed because I felt that I shouldn't have said that" (6). Once again, Meursault interprets an action (the caretaker's silence) as criticism when Camus gives no indication that it is intended to be so. Indeed, Meursault comments immediately afterwards that the caretaker asks why he does not want to see the body of his mother "without criticizing, as if he just wanted to know" (6). It is becoming clear to the reader that Meursault goes through his life faking the emotions, actions, and reactions which he senses that others will find appropriate, yet he frequently feels uneasy because of his inability to do so convincingly.

The close attentions of the caretaker, "this presence breathing down my neck," are beginning to annoy Meursault

(7). However, when the man offers to leave him, Meursault realizes that he will be alone with his mother's body and thus unable to avoid self-reflection. Despite his conscious intention to indicate to the caretaker that he may leave, Meursault gives the man the impression that he should stay, "I don't know what kind of gesture I made, but he stayed" (7). Clearly, Meursault's body language has given the wrong social cues, resulting in the opposite outcome from the one he consciously intended, another indication at once of Meursault's willingness to play the social game and his ineptness in so doing.

Applying his normal avoidance strategies when faced with the pressures of social intercourse, Meursault first distracts himself by noting physical sensations (the way the room is "filled with beautiful late-afternoon sunlight" and the sound of "[t]wo hornets buzzing against the glass roof") and then begins to feel himself "getting sleepy" (7). However, he accidentally diverts the conversation onto an acceptable topic by asking how long the caretaker has worked at the home, and, once the man begins to talk about how he came to his position at Marengo, Meursault ceases to feel oppressed by his presence; this topic makes no emotional demands since it deals exclusively with practical details. He recalls the caretaker's earlier contrast between the length of vigils in Paris and in Algeria and his explanation that the difference is based on the rates of human decomposition in the two climates. The caretaker's wife had found this subject entirely inappropriate and had reprimanded her husband who had "blushed and apologized" for his insensitivity (8). However, Meursault had felt no impropriety because he typically makes no value judgments and is interested in things that appeal to his intellect, "I thought what he had been saying was interesting and made sense" (8). Here, the reader sees again Meursault's fascination with logistical details; he does not recognize when the caretaker commits a social blunder because, although he is forced to conform to the protocol of formal grieving, it means nothing to him.

Expressions of Grief:

As the reader would expect, Meursault has no empathy for the grief of the other residents of the Marengo home: he seems to view the rest of humanity as a different species and himself as a disengaged observer. Upon his first encounter with them as he crosses the courtyard with the director, he describes their conversation as "like the muffled jabber of parakeets" a simile which denies meaning to the words spoken by the old people by suggesting that they are nothing more than a learned response repeated at appropriate times rather than genuine communication (5).

Meursault's experience of the vigil itself is dominated by the clash between negative and positive sense impressions. When the caretaker turns on the lights, the white light appears to attack him, "I was blinded by the sudden flash of light … every object, every angle and curve stood out so sharply it made by eyes hurt" (8-9). This description, another example of Meursault's projection of his psychological tension in a social situation onto the physical environment, prefigures the even greater discomfort he later feels on several occasions from the heat and glare of the sun. In contrast to the effect of the light, Meursault is pleased when the caretaker offers to bring him a coffee with milk because, as he says, "I like milk in my coffee" (8). The faux pas he commits here is that whilst society will approve of him drinking black coffee in order to help him to stay awake (the caretaker specifically mentions going to fetch black coffee for the others at the vigil), society will strongly disapprove of a grieving son drinking coffee simply for the pleasure of drinking coffee. The matter is brought up later at his trial as further evidence that Meursault is a monster when the prosecutor argues that "'a stranger may offer a cup of coffee, but … beside the body of the one who brought him into the world, a son should have refused it'" (91).

Having drunk the coffee, Meursault feels "like having a smoke," but even he recognizes that this might be seen as a little disrespectful though he quickly concludes that "it didn't

36

matter" (8). Once again, society will not concur with this judgment (the action will also be raised as evidence against Meursault at his trial), but the novel presents Meursault as right: *where* could it possibly matter? Nevertheless, it is a sign of Meursault's insecurity that he offers a cigarette to the caretaker as though his acceptance of it validates his own reasoning. Made drowsy by the combination of the hurtful glare of the white light and the pleasant sensations of the coffee, the cigarette and the smell of the flowers in the night air, Meursault falls to sleep, an avoidance strategy he uses whenever he is either physically or emotionally uncomfortable.

Woken by the rustling of the entrance of the other mourners, Maman's friends, Meursault feels distinctly uncomfortable: the whiteness of the room is now blindingly bright, there is no place which is in shadow, and "every object, every angle and curve stood out so sharply it made my eyes hurt" (9). Since white is a color traditionally associated with death and mourning, it is Meursault's confrontation with the reality of his own mortality which is being described by Camus as well as his need to externalize that confrontation. The description personifies inanimate objects, making them appear to be malicious; Meursault actually feels himself to be under attack by his physical environment. He perceives the mourners as a unit rather than as ten individuals: they move together and sit down together.

The description is dominated by the opposition of the two pronouns "they" and "I," and ironically Meursault now feels that *he* is the one being observed as though he is an entirely different species which reinforces the division which he feels between himself and others and again stresses his insecurity. At first, he does not recognize the ten mourners as people at all, "they floated into the blinding light without a sound" (9). The metaphor presents the old people as disembodied entities which become a part of the environment that is attacking him. He observes them as minutely as he did the room and with the same lack of humanity. Noting their grotesque appearance, he finds it hard "to believe they really existed" (9). There is a failure of empathy here, a failure to recognize the humanity of others, as though Meursault entirely lacks the essential elements that make us human.

Despite the fact that he correctly recognizes that in nodding their heads towards him the other mourners are greeting him, Meursault perceives the mourners as a jury "grouped around the caretaker ... It was then that I realized they were all sitting across from me, nodding their heads ... For a second I had the ridiculous feeling that they were there to judge me" (10). Meursault is once again externalizing his own sense of guilt. His perception of the old people is "ridiculous" in the same way that his earlier misperceptions about his boss and the director are ridiculous. The description does, however, foreshadow Meursault's trial where the prosecutor will say of him that "a man who is morally guilty of killing his mother severs himself from society" (101-102).

Meursault has already to a large extent severed his connection with society. Thus when one of the women begins "crying softly, steadily, in little sobs," he is simply irritated by the sound, and, although he is aware that it would be inappropriate to complain, he is glad when the woman "finally shut up" (10 and 11). In the contrast of diction between Meursault's delicate description of the woman's quiet crying and the brusqueness of his reaction, Camus presents his protagonist's reaction as selfish and unreasonable, a point which is reinforced when Meursault records that when the crying stops he is equally irritated by the fact that the mourners are not making any sound.

When the vigil ends, the old people surprise Meursault by shaking his hand as they leave. Meursault finds the gesture meaningless commenting mockingly that the old people are acting "as if that night during which we hadn't exchanged so much as a single word had somehow brought us closer together" (12). His sarcasm is concentrated into the incredulous phrase "as if" which denies the entire basis of the common humanity which the old people are seeking to claim; this underscores how utterly detached Meursault feels from society.

Mortality – the Ultimate Reality

Human mortality is the central theme of this chapter: all humans are subject to aging, disease and death, and there is nothing they can do about it. The theme is introduced, of course, in the novel's first sentence, "Maman died today," but it is also exemplified through the setting of the old people's home and the characters of the mourners, the caretaker, the Arab nurse and Thomas Perez (3). As has been noted, Meursault subjects the ten or so old people who come to his mother's vigil to the same intense scrutiny that he gives to the room. His grotesquely comic description of the "huge stomachs" of the old women, the "nest of wrinkles" which completely hide their eyes, and the lips sucked in by "toothless mouths" implicitly distances the old people from himself, a handsome man in his twenties (10). In his determination to distance himself from these people, Meursault ignores Hamlet's injunction in the graveyard scene, "Get you to my lady's chamber and tell her, let her paint an inch thick, to this favor she must come" – Meursault ignores it, but Camus knows that the reader will not (Hamlet 5.1).

Exactly like Meursault, the caretaker, who is sixty-four, maintains a distinction between himself and the residents of the home. He does so by clinging to the fiction of the official position which he gained after coming to the home because he was "destitute" (8). When Meursault points out that, despite the fact that he is employed as caretaker, he is "even so ... a resident," the caretaker objects vociferously calling the residents "'they'" or "'the others'" and, less often, "'the old people'" which makes no sense since, as Meursault points out, he is as old as many of them (8). However, to admit that he is like the residents would be to admit his own mortality; the caretaker copes with what the chaplain will later call the "'terrifying ordeal'" of the prospect of his own death in exactly the same way that Meursault does - by denying it (117). This is the first of a number of references in the novel to characters who simply attempt to deny the aging process and hence their own mortality.

The Arab nurse in a white smock suffers from a cancerous abscess which has eaten away her nose. As a result, "Where her nose should have been, the bandage was flat. All you could see of her face was the whiteness of the bandage" which recalls the shroud covering a dead woman (7). Thus, the nurse symbolizes the death which awaits everyone, and in looking at her face Meursault is forced to confront the disturbing truth which he avoids by not looking into the face of his dead mother. Significantly, Meursault is brought face to face with the nurse, whose silence is another link with "Maman," immediately after he has expressed his wish not to look at his mother's body.

Perez, the fiancée of Madam Meursault, is described as a grotesquely comic figure, and again, Meursault does this to distance himself from the mortality which Perez represents. On first seeing him, Meursault describes him as an "embarrassed-looking old man" (14). His appearance is clown-like, "trousers that were corkscrewed around his ankles ... a black tie with a knot that was too small ... a nose dotted with blackheads. Strange, floppy, thick-rimmed ears ... [of] blood-red color next to the pallor of his face" (14-15). This description is as sinister as it is comic, particularly when the reader realizes that Perez is Everyman: he is the fate which awaits all of us should we survive long enough. Three colors are repeatedly associated with death in this chapter: black, white and red, and these are the colors which appear in Meursault's description of Perez who has "blackheads" on his nose, "blood-red" ears, "white" hair and a pallid face (15).

Perez is the only character attending the funeral apart from Meursault who is not an authority figure; he is the only character who grieves openly and honestly for the death of the woman who was his friend. Seen in this context, Perez's desperate attempts to keep up with the funeral procession become a symbol for life: we all struggle to keep ahead of our ageing, using every ounce of our strength and every trick and short cut that our experience has taught us, but we inevitably fall behind. In the end, like Perez, we simply crumple "like a rag doll" (18). Meursault's description is cruelly mocking because he feels no empathy with this man, yet ironically he is closer to Perez than he is to any other character in this chapter. This, however, is something which Meursault will not realize until, following his final epiphany, he comes to understand the true nature of his mother's relationship with Perez. (The source of Maman's relationship with Perez is probably autobiographical. At the age of forty-eight, Camus' widowed mother, Catherine, had an affair with a married man which was brought to an abrupt end by the violent objections of Catherine's brother Etienne. It appears that Camus' older brother Lucien defended his mother, and that, in retrospect, Camus regretted not having taken the same position (Lottman 21-22]).

The descriptions of these three characters prefigure that of Salamano's dog: Salamano will vainly try every medicine and salve in order to cure his dog from the scabs which make his skin hideously ugly, but they cannot be cured because they are the inevitable accompaniment of old age. Perez exemplifies the truth of the nurse's statement to Meursault and of his comment upon it, "'If you go slowly, you risk getting sunstroke. But if you go too fast, you work up a sweat and then catch a chill inside the church.' She was right. There was no way out" (17). The nurse appears to be describing the dilemma presented by the heat of the sun, which is inescapable, and the contrasting chill of the church, but her words provide a symbol of the human condition which Meursault instinctively understands. Though no philosopher and not normally given to reflection, Meursault's comment encapsulates the human predicament which he has sought to deny throughout the chapter: he has been dying from the first moment he was born; it is only a matter of time.

Preparations for the Walk to the Church:

From the point at which the vigil breaks up to the moment that he leaves his mother's grave-side, Meursault is confronted by two hostile realities. The first is the official nature of the religious ceremony, and the second is the knowledge of his own mortality which the funeral of Maman forces upon him; the result of this dual confrontation is that he "becomes progressively less able to face death as the chapter goes on" (McCarthy 31). We have noted Meursault's surprise when the director informs him that Maman's friends said that his mother "often expressed … her desire for a religious funeral" because he remembers her as being, though nominally a Catholic, fundamentally uninterested in religion (6). Despite his certainty on this issue, and despite his own atheism (which becomes clear later in the novel), Meursault knows that he is literally powerless to change the arrangements which have already been made and makes no effort to do so. He is "told that the director was asking for me" and goes to see him; in his office, the director "had me sign a number of documents" (12, 12-13). Notice that Meursault is essentially passive here, subservient to the will of the representative of the state. The director, "dressed in black with pin-striped trousers," the uniform of authority, asks him if he "'would … like to see your mother one last time'" and in doing so makes the assumption that Meursault has already viewed the body, which we know not to be true (13). Next, the director sits down behind his desk (which symbolizes his official position) and explains the decisions which he has taken about the funeral: Maman's friends (he calls them "residents"), who were "let" keep the vigil, are not "allowed to attend"; he has given Thomas Perez special "permission" to attend, though "on the advice of our visiting physician" he was barred from the vigil; and he has notified the priest (13). Everything has been taken out of Meursault's hands. Outside, Meursault encounters the priest, the second authority figure in this chapter to assume a paternal relationship by calling him "'my son,'" who is "adjusting the length of" the silver chain on the censer" (13). Meursault's relationship with the priest is encapsulated in one sentence,

"He went inside; I followed" (13). The authorities have marginalized Meursault, made him an outsider, a mere observer at his own mother's burial – as marginalized here as he will later feel himself to be at his own trial.

Once the casket is taken outside, Meursault feels events to move forward in a way beyond his control, "From then on everything happened very quickly" (13). Everything is in the hands of other people, as can be seen by the changing subjects of Meursault's sentences, "The director ... The men ... The priest ... A woman," which reflect the way in which his consciousness is being bombarded by impressions (13). It is at this point that Meursault's tone changes abruptly: his language, which has always been personal, now for the first time becomes the language of dissent as he mocks the absurdity of the ceremony in which he is being forced to participate, "Varnished, glossy, and oblong, it [the hearse] reminded me of a pencil box" (13). The comparison derides the pretentions of the ceremony by reducing its centerpiece to the level of a cheap box designed to hold nothing more important than a pencil. Notice that Meursault's sarcasm is not directed at his mother's body but at what society is doing to her body. That this is the focus of Meursault's dissent is made clear by his description of the funeral director as "a little man in a ridiculous getup" (13).

A Walk in the Sun:

Catherine Brosman writes that, "Camus's Romanticism is evidenced primarily in his use of nature as a correlative of human feeling (what the English aesthetician John Ruskin labeled and criticized as 'the pathetic fallacy')" (56). Indeed, in order to understand *The Stranger*, it is essential to understand the significance of nature, and particularly of the sun, because on three occasions sunlight and its associated heat impact Meursault's feelings and actions in crucial ways. These occasions are: the walk to the grave, the shooting of the Arab, and the interrogations by court officials. There have been many attempts to explain the significance of sun motif in the novel: the sun represents death, the father, the mother, etc. Having

43

reviewed a number of interpretations, Patrick McCarthy concludes, "There is in *The Stranger* no consistent view of the sun" and again, "The sun remains an image and eludes close definition" (33 and 35). If this is true, then *The Stranger* is a fundamentally flawed work since Camus certainly appears to present the sun as having a consistent meaning.

The morning of the funeral begins well for Meursault, which is to say that his experience of it is dominated by pleasant sense impressions. There is taste, "I had some more coffee with milk, which was very good"; sight, "the sky was streaked with red"; touch "the wind coming over the hills"; and smell, "the smell of salt ... the smell of fresh earth" (12). Meursault is convinced that, "It was going to be a beautiful day. I could feel how much I'd enjoy going for a walk if it hadn't been for Maman" (12). What is it (apart from the realistic description of the unbearable heat of Algeria in summer) that turns the day into a torment for Meursault?

The key to the answer is that the sun is not a symbol to Camus; rather, it is (unconsciously) symbolic *to* Meursault. Just as Meursault projects his feelings of guilt onto other people, assuming that they are judging him and condemning him because he feels guilty, so Meursault anthropomorphizes the sun: when he is feeling good about life, he perceives the sun as benevolent, and when he is feeling bad about life, he perceives the sun as malevolent. Either way, he is making a huge error, but this is something which he (and the reader) will only come to understand after his epiphany at the end of the novel. This interpretation accounts for the inconsistency in the meaning of the sun through the novel which McCarthy notes: the inconsistency, which is an indication that he is making a mistake, belongs to Meursault, not to Camus.

We have already analyzed how, as preparations for the walk to the grave are made, Meursault is increasingly confronted by the authority figures representative of society's norms. It is significant that as he feels himself to be losing his identity, the power of the sun appears to him to gradually increase. As he waits in the courtyard, Meursault notes, "The sun was now a little higher in the sky; it was beginning to warm my feet" (12). There is nothing negative in this sentence, but following his discussion with the director, his introduction to the priest, and his description of Perez, the tone changes, "The sky was already filled with light. The sun was beginning to bear down on the earth and it was getting hotter by the minute … the sun bearing down … [was] making the whole landscape shimmer with heat, it was inhuman and oppressive" (15). In these sentences the sun is personified: it appears to be acting independently and deliberately.

The change in Meursault's perception results from, on the one hand, his sense of alienation from all of those around him who seem to be committed to a ceremony which he finds meaningless and even comic, and, on the other hand, the fact that he is being forced to confront the reality of his own mortality. At this point, the director tells Meursault about his mother's walks to the village in the evening with Perez, and Meursault contrasts her experience then with his own now. The colors which he associates with these evening walks are the vibrant, life colors red and green, and he instinctively feels that Maman's relationship with the sun was different from his own, "… the houses standing out here and there against the red and green earth. I was able to understand Maman better. Evenings in that part of the country must have been a kind of sad relief" (15). For a moment, Meursault catches a glimpse of what he will only come to understand at the end of the narrative: that once one has accepted the reality of one's own death, then one understands man's true relationship with the world (and, necessarily, with the sun). Reconciled with one's own mortality, the world is perceived neither as benevolent nor malevolent and, to quote McCarthy's alternative translation of the final sentence of the above quotation, "In this region evening must be a melancholy truce" (33). Evening symbolizes old age when death can no longer be ignored but must be accepted as imminent, and thus the struggle is ended.

For Meursault, however, there is no truce. He is doubly alienated being both a stranger to the society which seeks to make him conform and a man desperately trying to deny his very mortality. As the procession begins to move forward, Meursault has another confrontation with one of society's anonymous representatives in the form of the "man from the undertaker's" (16). Undoubtedly meaning to be sympathetic, the man attempts to open a conversation, "He pointed up at the sky and repeated, 'Pretty hot.' I said, 'Yes.' A minute later he asked, 'Is that your mother in there?' Again I said 'Yes.' 'Was she old?' I answered, 'Fairly,' because I did not know the exact number. After that he was quiet" (16). Meursault's monosyllabic answers and agreement with the speaker are further examples of his use of avoidance strategies when he wishes to end an uncomfortable conversation, but there is more to the exchange that this for it serves both to distance Meursault further from society and to bring him closer to confronting the meaning of his mother's death.

The undertaker's man (like Meursault's boss in the next chapter) wants to know Maman's age, and, when he gets the assurance that she is fairly old, he (like Meursault's boss when he is told that Maman was, "'[a]bout sixty'" [25]) feels reassured. This illustrates the way in which society regards length of life as being significant: Maman's death is more acceptable because she had a good long life, whilst the death of a young person would me much more sorrowful. Meursault, however, does not calculate life in this way. Of course, he does not know his mother's age partly because he has not been close to her for some time, but more fundamentally because for Meursault the significant thing about death is not *when* it happens but *that* it happens. Once again, the mechanisms which society uses to gloss over the significance of death are irrelevant to Meursault. On the other hand, the man's question whether it is Maman's body in the coffin inevitably brings home the reality of death to Meursault, and so his feeling that the sun is attacking him grows, "All around me there was still the same glowing countryside flooded with sunlight. The glare

46

from the sky was unbearable" (16). What is actually "unbearable" is the inevitability of his own death.

Meursault is now assailed by a succession of negative sensual experiences. The tar on the road has "burst open in the sun," and Meursault feels his feet sink into it as into the "pulp" of fruit (16 and 17), and the coachman's black hat appears to be made of "the same black mud" as the road (17). The word "black' occurs five times in two sentences; it literally appears to Meursault to be the only color since he refers to "the monotony of the colors around me" (17). Next Meursault describes Perez grotesque dance of death as he tries unavailingly to keep up with the procession. In a description which foreshadows Meursault's feelings just before he shoots the Arab, he tells us, "All of it – the sun, the smell of leather and horse dung from the hearse, the smell of varnish and incense, and my fatigue after a night without sleep – was making it hard for me to see or think straight … I could feel the blood pounding in my temples" (17). The reader can clearly see that Meursault is here projecting his alienation from the funeral ritual onto the smell of the leather, the horse, the varnish, and the incense, just as he is projecting his despair at his own mortality onto the heat and the sun. It is, as McCarthy correctly comments, an "hallucination … [which] compels Meursault to flee" from the grave-side (31).

The Return to Routine:

The chapter ends with a list of images from the day of the funeral. Meursault says not that he remembered them but that they have "stuck in my mind" which stresses his passivity and suggests that the images have some sort of independent existence (18). As we might expect, the images are sense impressions: sounds, "voices … the incessant drone of the motor"; textures, "all the wrinkles … they [his tears] spread out and ran together, leaving a watery film over his ruined face"; and, above all, colors, "the red geraniums on the graves … the blood-red earth, the white flesh of the roots" (18). Meursault, hyper-sensitive as ever to his environment, appears to have no explanation for the memorable nature of these images, but to the reader they symbolize the inevitable and uneven battle between life and death, red representing life-blood and white the funeral shroud and the lifeless bones of the corpse. The villagers who Meursault notices on the sidewalks beside the church will soon join Maman in the graveyard, and their faith (real or pretended) in religion, represented by the church, will prove neither a protection nor a consolation: time will ruin them all. Their fate (and ours) is symbolized by Perez collapsing "like a rag doll" a simile which robs him of his humanity as death robs us of our humanity (18).

Ironically, Meursault feels emotion for the first time when "the nest of lights that was Algiers" seen from the bus moves him to "joy" (18). The metaphor carries connotations of birth, nurturing, protection and security. For Meursault, however, the image does not suggest his mother but rather the tranquility of the life he lived in the years between Maman entering the Marengo home and the arrival of the telegram. In the normal routine of life, Meursault hopes that he will rediscover a sanctuary from the emotional demands of social interaction and his delight in the summer sun. In the short-term Algiers offers the refuge of twelve hours' sleep.

Summary:

Meursault is an office worker not a philosopher; as he later tells his lawyer, he has "pretty much lost the habit of analyzing [himself]" (65).

Meursault is the narrator and protagonist in the novel. He is not Camus and neither is he Camus' spokesman.

Meursault narrates his story just before his execution at a point where he understands its full significance, but his aim in the narrative is (with very few exceptions) to convey accurately his feelings at the time things happened.

Meursault is not '"the same as anyone"' much as he would like others to believe that he is (67).

Meursault's inability to feel emotion is not a result of a psychological illness.

Meursault regards emotions as meaningless abstractions – fictions invented by people to make themselves feel better by giving their lives the appearance of meaning.

Deeply aware that he has a different world view from everyone else, Meursault spends most of his time trying to read other people in order to know what is expected of him.

Meursault frequently misreads social situations causing him to feel embarrassed, inadequate and even guilty.

Meursault experiences life as a succession of unconnected sensual experiences, some pleasant and some unpleasant.

PART ONE Chapter 2: Killing Time

> For I have known them all already, known them all:
> Have known the evenings, mornings, afternoons,
> I have measured out my life with coffee spoons;
> (T. S. Eliot "The Love Song of J. Alfred Prufrock")

Consider the following:

1. As the chapter opens, Meursault suddenly thinks that he understands why his boss was annoyed that he asked for two days off work. Comment on his use of the following expressions:

a) "why my boss had seemed annoyed" (19);

b) "naturally, my boss thought" (19);

c) "that still doesn't keep me from understanding my boss's point of view" (19).

Find other examples in this chapter of Meursault apparently coming to an understanding of the feelings of other people.

2. Comment on the way in which Meursault describes his attraction for Marie, "I'd had a thing for her at the time" (19). How did he react to the end of their relationship?

3. What leads Meursault to comment of Marie, "she seemed very surprised" [Note that word "seemed" again!] and, "[s]he gave a little start" (20)? Comment on Meursault's statement that his mother died, "'Yesterday'" (20). How does he respond when he notes Marie's reaction?

4. How does Meursault's description of his interactions with Marie on the beach and in the cinema indicate the importance he places on the physical aspects of existence?

5. Do you find Meursault's behavior on the day after his mother's funeral inappropriate? Why (or why not)?

6. What seems to you significant about the way in which Meursault describes the people who he observes from his balcony? How is Meursault different from the "distinguished" man with his wife and children, the waiter doing his job, and the young soccer players (23)?

7. Comment on the sentence, "Then I thought maybe I ought to have some dinner" (24). What does it show about Meursault?

8. Based on your reading of this chapter, why do you think that Meursault does not like Sundays?

Misreading Motivation

The chapter opens with one of those frequent misinterpretations of the actions of others to which Meursault is prone, "my boss had seemed annoyed when I asked him for two days off" (19). The word "seemed" is often used by Meursault; it describes his attempts to read the actions of others, reminding us that, since he does not instinctively understand emotions, he is forced to deduce a person's feelings based on external observation. Here, he misinterprets his boss's seriousness and sympathy for anger, and this leads to a convoluted chain of reasoning which the reader finds comic because it is based on a patently false assumption. Meursault finds a logistical reason for his boss's supposed anger in the fact that, since the funeral was going to be on a Friday, Meursault had asked for Thursday and Friday off work thus giving himself a four-day weekend. This mathematical reasoning allows Meursault to understand his "boss's point of view" (19). Ironically, he feels more empathy with his boss than he did with the mourners at the vigil; anger at two days' lost productivity seems entirely reasonable to Meursault, whereas weeping over a death seems pointless. Nevertheless, he still feels the need to defend himself on the grounds that, firstly, it was not his "fault if they buried Maman yesterday," and secondly, that he "would have had Saturday and Sunday off anyway" (19). The comedy of the first paragraph is encapsulated in the single adverbs "naturally" and "[o]bviously" which both convey Meursault's naïve confidence in his ability to interpret the feelings of others at the very moment when the narrative shows the reader that he is making a ludicrous misjudgment. The fact that Camus uses comic irony in his presentation of Meursault's reasoning is further evidence that the reader is not to mistake the views of the narrator/ protagonist for those of the author.

Work-time and Free-time

The novel tells us little about Meursault's job. He seems to be a shipping clerk - that is, to have a job which involves administration rather than production and therefore has no visible end-product. In this sense, the work which Meursault does is a microcosm of the world in which he lives: there is no obvious point to either. Camus seems to have based Meursault's situation largely on his own experience of working during a school vacation in the office of a maritime broker where he filed mail and bills, translated lists of provisions, and visited customs offices. Olivier Todd sums up the impact which this vacation job had on Camus who quickly became bored with this work:

> At the office, Camus learned about administrative jobs, where one rarely sees the results of one's efforts – "this office work which comes from nowhere and ends up with nothing. Everything revolved around buying and selling, mediocre actions which were impossible to appreciate." His uncle Etienne's barrel workshop required skilled hands, and a new barrel could be admired or rejected. Albert developed the idea of a worker as an artisan who made an object. (15)

Nothing more clearly illustrates the gulf in intellectual development between Camus and his protagonist, for

Meursault finds no fault with his work at the office and has no desire to gain promotion to a position which would give him more freedom and control during his working hours. In fact, Meursault is a good worker, and he enjoys his work; he will later record with satisfaction, "I worked hard all week" (34). At work, he is not a stranger because, like everyone else, his time is not his own. He works under the direction of his boss who makes all of the meaningful decisions; Meursault's function is to take care of practical details, which he does very efficiently. A Marxist would speak of 'alienation' since a clerical worker does not create a product that he then sells to a real person but simply sells his labor for a wage; however, work is ironically the one place Meursault does not feel alienated, and the boss will later mistakenly offer him a promotion based on the good impression which he has created.

Weekends are uncomfortable for Meursault precisely because they lack the routine and the sense of order which he enjoys at work. Above all, weekends mean that he has to fill his time, and this is not easy for him. Whilst most people look forward to the freedom of the weekend, Meursault finds himself in an uncomfortable dilemma precisely because he has to make decisions about how to spend his time, "I wondered what I was going to do" (19). Not surprisingly, Meursault opts for physical activity, and a chance encounter at the beach with a former co-worker, Marie Cardona, allows him to pass his Saturday pleasantly enough, but, since Marie has something to do on Sunday, that day stretches before him like a wasteland, "I remembered that it was Sunday, and that bothered me: I don't like Sundays" (21). A detailed examination of Meursault's description of how he spends the Saturday and Sunday following his mother's funeral shows how truly limited and inauthentic his existence is.

Sensual Gratification

Meursault's relationship with Marie is, on his part and initially on hers, purely physical. The reader has seen that he is unnaturally appreciative of pleasant sensations and unnaturally averse to unpleasant sensations; Marie Cardona exclusively provides the former. Meursault explains his earlier relationship with her by saying, "I'd had a thing for [her] at the time. She did too, I think. But she'd left soon afterwards and we didn't have the time" (19). His use of the (at the time) common euphemism "thing" indicates both that his attraction to her was based on sexual attraction and that it went no further than this. Blaming the fact that the relationship never developed on Marie's leaving the office is a further example of Meursault's dishonesty since it is perfectly clear that Meursault did not pursue the relationship with Marie for the same reason that he did not visit his mother at Marengo: to do either would have required the motivation provided by emotional attachment, and just as Meursault felt no emotional attachment for Maman, he felt (and will continue to feel) none for Marie.

The reunion with Marie is completely fortuitous. Meursault comments that he "ran into Marie" using language which makes the meeting sound random and inconsequential (19). From the first moment, it is clear that Meursault's attraction to Marie is based on sensuality. No description of Marie is given; she appears to exist only in terms of the physical effects (predominantly touch) which she has on Meursault. He says, "I brushed across her breasts," the alliteration stressing the tactile sensation (20). When he rests his head on her stomach, he notes that he, "could feel Marie's heart beating softly" (20). His description of Marie is like an inventory of body parts, "breasts … stomach …waist … leg," and yet the reader is left with no idea what Marie actually looks like other than a general impression that she is a beautiful young woman (20). Meursault's pleasure in Marie's body, as we have now come to expect, is projected onto his perception of the physical environment, "I had the whole sky in my eyes and it was blue and gold" (20). Colors suggesting beauty and value have replaced the life/death colors red, white and black which dominated Chapter One. When the sun does become "too hot," they both dive into the sea to get cool (20).

It has not occurred to Meursault that his behavior in making a pass at Marie might be seen as inappropriate. Because he does not see his mother's death as part of a meaningful structure of human existence, Meursault makes no connection between it and his interaction with Marie. However, he is reminded of social conventions when Marie sees his black tie, and he notes that "she seemed very surprised" (20). The use of the word "seemed" stresses once again that Meursault is forced to rely on observing the reactions of other people to judge their feelings. Perhaps because of his embarrassment, Meursault uses his normal strategy of answering by saying the thing which is easiest for him even if it is not the truth: in reply to her question, he tells Marie that Maman died on Friday which was actually the day of her funeral. Unfortunately for Meursault, this lie has the effect of making his actions seem even more inappropriate, and draws a more extreme reaction from Marie who "gave a little start" (20). Typically, Meursault interprets this as criticism and feels the urge to defend himself until he remembers that this is a repeat of a conversation which he has had with his boss. His final comment, "you always feel a little guilty" shows Meursault once more trying to convince himself that he is "the same as anyone" (67). This is, in fact, not true. Meursault's conduct defines him as a stranger to social norms; he feels guilty because he is aware that his failure to grieve for his mother is socially unacceptable and that society would condemn him for it.

In becoming involved with Marie, Meursault unwittingly gets himself into a situation which will come to mirror his relationship with his mother. Initially this seems unlikely since Marie appears to be motivated by solely physical desire. Patrick McCarthy's translation of Meursault's account of their previous relationship makes this very clear, "[Marie] was a typist in my office and at the time I wanted her. She wanted me too, I believe" (35). On either side the motivation was the desire to have sex. At the beach, Marie is not put off by the knowledge that Meursault is in mourning for his mother despite her initial shock. She has "forgotten all about it" by evening, sees no reason to change her initial plan that they should go to a comedy film. It is she who "had her leg pressed against" Meursault's whilst he is "fondling her breasts" (20). Near the end of the movie, Meursault comments that, "I gave her a kiss, but not a good one" (20). He evaluates the success of the kiss on purely physical criteria; emotions are not involved. It seems that he has found someone who, like him, lives in the moment for the sensual gratification of the moment, but this will change.

Killing Time

Without Marie, this Sunday (like every other Sunday) is a void, more so even than usual because Meursault does not go to Celeste's since he knows that he will be made uncomfortable by questions about his mother's funeral, "and I don't like that" (21). He approaches the task of filling this void in a very negative frame of mind, "I don't like … I don't feel like … I don't like … I didn't feel like" (21). As the reader might by now expect, Meursault uses two avoidance strategies: he stays in bed all morning and seeks sensual gratification by chain-smoking. He cannot even summon up the motivation to go downstairs to buy some bread. Camus initially sketched out this episode in December 1937 in a way which makes it clear that the reader should see his existence as purely passive and therefore inauthentic, "On Sundays, he gets up very late and stands in the window, watching the sun or the rain, the passers-by or the silent street. He is waiting for death" (*Carnets* quoted in Gay-Crosier 51).

There still remains the long afternoon. Meursault is "a little bored … I wandered around the apartment," the word "wandered" suggesting his lack of direction and motivation, and "just for something to do" he reads an old newspaper (21). One way that Meursault passes his time is by cutting things out of the newspaper which "interest" him and sticking them in an

56

old notebook (21). The reader noted in Chapter One Meursault's tendency to find things interesting rather than to respond to them with emotion. In that case, it was the rate of decomposition of dead bodies related to climate, and in this case he is interested by an advertisement for Kruschen Salts, a preparation used to relieve constipation and regulate the bowel. Both, of course, relate to exclusively to the physical aspect of life and death.

Meursault comments that the apartment, which "was just the right size when Maman was here ... [is] too big" for him since her death and that he now lives in only "one room ... with some saggy straw chairs, a wardrobe whose mirror has gone yellow, a dressing table, and a brass bed" (21). Camus here presents the reader with a symbol of Meursault's inauthentic life: the world has much more to offer than Meursault is capable of appreciating and experiencing. If the mother is seen to represent the feminine side of Meursault's personality, the emotional side, then his action in placing her in the home is seen as a deliberate rejection of one side of his personality. Without his mother, he is no longer complete: he is an unaware man who has reduced living to a succession of physical sensations. Only in the epiphany which he has right at the end of the novel will he understand this and in doing so reconnect with his mother.

Meursault spends the afternoon on his balcony observing those who have no problems filling their free time, people who clearly attach great importance to the social activities (family outings, team games, etc.) in which they are engaged. There are no individuals; people are all in groups, "families ... local boys ... gangs of fans ... [the soccer] team ... moviegoers ... local girls ... young men" (21-24). (The reference to soccer fans serves to remind the reader of the distinction between author and protagonist: Camus was an enthusiastic and skillful soccer player keeping goal for the Racing Universitaire d'Alger team from 1928 to 1930 when ill-health ended his playing days.) Meursault understands that it is in these social groupings that people find a sense of identity and purpose: it is the role of husband and father which turns the "rather frail little man" into a person regarded by the people of the neighborhood as "distinguished" (22), and it is being in the team which has the players "shouting and singing at the tops of their lungs" (23). However, these are groups from which Meursault excludes himself even when they appear to be trying to include him. Thus, when the soccer players wave and call to him that they won, he can only nod "as if to say 'Yes'" – once more he is conscious of faking an involvement which he does not feel. When some of the young girls who he knows wave to him, he makes no response. Meursault uses the pronoun 'they' eight times on page twenty-three to differentiate himself from the people whose lives he is watching. His isolation on the balcony from the life of the community is a perfect symbol of Meursault as the voyeur, the stranger, and of the meaninglessness of his life.

In *The Myth of Sisyphus*, Camus writes, "A world that can be explained even with bad reasons is a familiar world. But, on the other hand, in a world suddenly divested of illusions and lights, man feels like an alien, a stranger" (6). Those who Meursault has been watching are at home in the world because their "illusions" and their "bad reasons" make it comfortable; Meursault, however, knows the "illusions" and "bad reasons" for what they are and so can find no comfortable role in the world because he lacks any reason to value life. Olivier Todd concludes that Meursault "was absurd because, among other things, he did not look for meaning in what happened to him. Instead, he abstained from commenting or judging" (Todd 146).

Meursault's observation is detailed and precise emphasizing colors, "pink … brown … red" (22) and textures, "wet and slippery … stiff clothes … greased … embroidered" (21-22). Pausing only to eat chocolate and to smoke (more sensual gratification), Meursault observes the changing weather with exactly the same detachment with which he observes people. Significantly, he feels the afternoon to be "beautiful," and at no time mentions the heat or the sun as being oppressive. In fact, the sky is "clear but dull," and later "the sky grew dark and I thought we were in for a summer storm" (22). Since he is entirely "comfortable" (22) sitting on his chair observing life which makes no emotional demands on him, he is at one with the physical world and "sat there for a long time and watched the sky" (23).

Meursault meticulously records each set of people returning from their Sunday activities: at five o'clock, the gangs of football fans; in the early evening, people "straggling back from their walks" (23); almost immediately afterwards, the ones who had gone to local cinemas and later those who had gone to the cinemas in town; and finally the young men and women promenading the streets. In a phrase made famous by Christopher Isherwood, Meursault might say of himself, "I am a camera" because, despite the efforts of society to draw Meursault in, he remains a voyeur. When evening falls, Meursault has dinner alone. What is significant, however, is the reason he gives for having dinner, "I thought maybe I ought to have dinner" (24). The use of the word "ought" is another indication of how vulnerable Meursault is to the pressure of social expectation; he eats because he knows that everyone else is eating, not because he is hungry.

The pronoun "I" is used nine times in the final paragraph of the chapter emphasizing again Meursault's isolation from those he has been observing (24). This is how he wants his life to be because there are no emotional demands upon him, and he finally concludes with satisfaction that "another Sunday was over, that Maman was buried now, that I was going back to work, and that, really, nothing had changed" (24). For Meursault, nothing has changed because his relationship with his mother has not changed since her death: she was effectively dead to him the moment she went into the home, so her actual death has no real significance. However, Meursault is making a crucial misjudgment. In fact, Maman's death has already begun a chain of events which will make it impossible for him to return to the idyllic world of emotionally undemanding routine which he has inhabited for several years. His relationship with Marie is just the first such event.

Summary:

Meursault feels most comfortable when he does not have to take decisions.

Meursault finds refuge from thought in practical details and logistics which explains both why he is happy in his work and why he is such an efficient and productive employee.

Meursault's experience of being alive is limited to life physical gratification and a daily routine of activities.

In Marie, Meursault appears to have found a companion who also lives exclusively for the gratification of her senses.

Meursault hates having free-time.

Meursault is no more capable of romantic love than he is capable of filial love.

Meursault is a stranger to the neighborhood in which he lives.

PART ONE Chapter 3: Friends

> Since God does not exist and man dies, everything is permissible. One experience is as good as another; the important thing is simply to acquire as many as possible. (Jean-Paul Sartre "An Explication of *The Stranger*")

Consider the following:

1. Meursault admits that he does not understand why his boss "seemed to be relieved" (25). What is it that he is failing to understand about his boss's behavior? What else about his boss does Meursault record without appearing to understand it? How does Meursault in a similar way fail to understand and respond appropriately to Celeste a little later in the chapter?

2. Meursault reports that his boss said that the wet towel is "really a minor detail" (25). Why is it not minor to Meursault?

3. What does the incident in which Meursault and Emannuel jump up on the truck tell us about Meursault? Look particularly at the language that is used to describe the incident.

4. Both Celeste and Raymond take a moral position on Salamano beating his dog. What is it? How does Meursault react?

5. Contrast the way in which "the neighborhood" regards Raymond with Meursault's attitude towards him. How do you explain the difference?

6. Why does Meursault agree to be Raymond's "pal"?

7. Raymond describes several acts of violence that he has committed. How does Camus bring home to the reader the seriousness of these through Raymond's own account? What is Meursault's reaction to hearing about them?

8. Why does Meursault agree to assist in Raymond's scheme to get revenge on his mistress? Comment on the use of adjectives in the following description, "he took out a sheet of paper, a *yellow* envelope, a *small red* pen box, and a *square* bottle with *purple* ink in it" (emphasis added 32).

9. At the end of the chapter, Meursault thinks, "[Raymond said] that it was one of those things that was bound to happen sooner or later. I thought so too" (33). What similarities, and what differences, do you find between the views of life and death held by Meursault and by Raymond?

Social Interactions:

Meursault is relieved to return to work; hard work obviates the need to take decisions, to take responsibility for those decisions, and to respond emotionally to others. However, Camus juxtaposes two examples of Meursault's inability to understand his boss to illustrate that, even in the sanctuary of a world dominated by practical tasks, human interaction intrudes on Meursault's consciousness. Firstly, he records that his boss is "nice" to him as though this is a random act of kindness and not, as the reader instinctively understands, an expression of support for Meursault's loss (25). When asked his mother's age, Meursault replies vaguely that she was around sixty because he does not want to repeat the embarrassment he suffered when he had to tacitly admit to the man from the undertaker that he "didn't know the exact number" (16). The boss's reaction to this information is, however, a mystery to Meursault, as he openly acknowledges, "I don't know why, but he seemed to be relieved somehow" (25). The reader understands that the boss feels that Meursault's mother had a reasonably long life and that some comfort can be taken in that, which is why the boss is able "to consider the matter closed" (25). However, even though he is not consciously aware of it, length of life is not the issue for Meursault; the inescapable fact of human mortality is the issue, so the issue can never be closed. This explains the failure of the two to communicate.

A second misunderstanding between Meursault and his boss occurs as a result of Meursault's hyper-sensitivity to sensual experience. Meursault contrasts the extreme pleasure which he gets from wiping his hands on a fresh, clean roller towel at lunchtimes with the disgust he feels at using that same towel later in the day when it is wet through use. To the boss this is "really a minor detail," but to Meursault it is vitally important because, in an existence stripped of values and emotions, sensual experience is the *only* thing he has left (25).

At Celeste's, Meursault once again fails to understand the significance of his friend's polite enquire "if things were 'all right now,'" replying in a socially inappropriate way, "I told him yes they were and said I was hungry" (26). Meursault interprets the inquiry as relating to the practical details of the funeral, completely missing the fact that it is an inquiry by a friend about his emotional state. A good meal, some wine, a siesta, a cigarette, an afternoon at work going through his "stack of freight invoices," and going home in the evening put Meursault in an excellent mood. He comments, "The sky was green; I felt good" (26). Here again the reader perceives Meursault falling into the fallacy "that man might indeed be part of a harmonious nature" (McCarthy 36).

Risk-taking

The incident in which Meursault and Emmanuel jump on the speeding truck foreshadows much that will happen later in the novel. It is important to note that it is Emmanuel who initiates the action, "Emmanuel said, 'How about it?' and I started running" (25). Having no self-motivation, Meursault is always vulnerable to strong-willed people, and here he acquiesces instantly, without a moment's thought, a characteristic which will repeatedly lead him to be drawn into dangerous situations. The danger of this particular action is compounded by the fact that Meursault entirely loses himself in the sensations of the activity, and thus his critical faculties cease to function, "I was engulfed by the noise and the dust … all I was conscious of was the sensation of hurling forward in a mad dash" (25-6). The word "engulfed" is significant because it conveys the degree to which Meursault becomes caught up in the activity which is "mad" not in the sense in which Meursault uses the word (i.e. hectic) but quite literally because the two men are recklessly risking their lives. Once again, the reckless way in which Meursault lives his life is determined by his view of the meaninglessness of life: for Meursault, in the words of the chaplain at the end of the novel "'when you die, you die, and nothing remains,'" which means that the time of death is not important; only the fact of death is important (117).

Love and Mortality

The description of Salamano and his dog going on their walk twice a day for eight years is grotesquely comic in a way that recalls the description of Thomas Perez. Firstly, there is the same emphasis on the ugliness of age, the skin of both master and dog being marked by "sores and scabs," and each having the same "stooped look" (26, 27). Secondly, there is the fact that, like Perez, they seem to make no progress as first "the old man … pulls the dog … [then the dog] starts dragging its master" which mirrors the alternating spurts and falling behind of Perez in his desperate efforts to keep up with the coffin (27). To Meursault, it appears that the man and the dog "hate each other," yet they do the same things every day and "haven't changed their route in eight years" (27). The emphasis on repetition calls to mind the curse of Sisyphus who is forced to roll a huge boulder up a steep hill, but each time he reaches the top, the massive stone would always roll back down, forcing him to begin again.

A more sinister aspect of the relationship is the violence which Salamano uses against the dog which foreshadows Raymond Sintès' coercive relationship with his mistress. The beatings are also a daily ritual which "has been going on for eight years" (27). Meursault observes this, but he fails to understand that Salamano's walking and beating of the dog are a habit, a routine (comparable to himself going to the office) which allows him to get through life without thinking about his disappointments and without thinking of his approaching death. This is made clear in the next chapter.

Meursault is unable to condemn Salamano's treatment of the dog which even Celeste finds to be "'pitiful'" (27). He only comments "really who's to say" (27). When Raymond Sintès uses the words "'pitiful'" and "disgusting" to describe Salamano's cruelty, Meursault replies that he does not find it so, which raises the whole issue of the viability of moral values in a world which has no place for transcendent values (28). Camus explains this point in *The Myth of Sisyphus* when he argues that, "No code of ethics and no effort are justifiable *a priori* in the face of the cruel mathematics that command our conditions" (16). Knowing this instinctively, Meursault feels that he has no basis upon which to condemn Salamano – no right to do so.

In the same way, he makes no moral judgment of the pimp Raymond Sintès, who is universally disliked in the neighborhood as a result of his immoral activities, because Meursault's personal contacts with the man have always been pleasant. Once again, for Meursault abstract moral concepts have no validity; the only thing that matters is immediate sensation, "he often talks to me ... I find what he has to say interesting" (28). What is non-threatening to Meursault about talking to Sintès is that the conversation is one-sided: Sintès talks and Meursault listens. Here the reader recalls that Meursault uses the word "interesting" to describe the caretaker's comments on the relative speed of human decomposition on the night of Maman's vigil. Such a reaction is only possible to someone for whom the moral context of a person's remarks is rendered meaningless by "the cruel mathematics" of human mortality.

A World without Values

The reader recognizes almost immediately that Raymond Sintès has a cynical motive for inviting Meursault to supper: he wishes to make him an accomplice in a criminal plot to take revenge on his "mistress" (29). Sintès is an immoral man who seeks power over others, and Meursault's mind-set makes him a willing tool. Camus clearly foreshadows Sintès' violent nature. Firstly, there is the reference to his "nose like a boxer's," then he offers to share his "blood sausage," and finally he bandages his injured hand (28). His room is described in typically male terms: it is "dirty and the bed ... unmade," and on the walls are pictures of male athletes ("boxers" [McCarthy 37]) and pinups of "naked women" hinting both at male violence and hostility to women (28).

The reader sees what Meursault observes but does not understand and is therefore easily manipulated: Sintès has been cultivating his acquaintance for some time, "he often talks to me and sometimes stops by my place for a minute," and the apparent casualness of Sintès' invitation to supper is forced and cynical, "'I've got some blood sausage and some wine at my place. How about joining me?'" (28). Meursault immediately accepts, seeing merely the immediate convenience of not having to cook his own supper.

Meursault judges only on the basis of personal experience saying of Sintès, "I don't have any reason not to talk to him" (28). To illustrate the limitations of this approach, Camus juxtaposes Meursault's accurate judgment of Sintès' bandage with his inability to judge Sintès' account of the fight that he has been in. Ironically, Meursault has no problem applying the term "dubious-looking" to the former because he means only that the bandage does not look clean or hygienic, whilst he is completely uncritical of Sintès' account of the fight and his patently self-serving conclusion that it was all the fault of his opponent. Meursault naively accepts Sintès' conclusion that the other man got what he deserved, "It was true and I agreed" (29). It simply never occurs to Meursault that Sintès could be lying.

The whole evening with Sintès is described as a male bonding session (in the next chapter Sintès will suggest that they visit a brothel together), and as such it is equivalent to

Meursault's heterosexual bonding with Marie; both will eventually place stressful emotional demands upon Meursault which are not evident at their commencement. Having no self-motivation and being entirely unaware of Sintès' cynical manipulation, Meursault is pathetically vulnerable to the highly-motivated Sintès and acquiesces because doing so seems to have no cost to himself, "I said it was fine by me; he seemed pleased" (29). He does not see the ulterior motives which Sintès has for wanting to be "pals" with him (29). A fatal weakness in Meursault's character is his desire to make other people happy, something which he does not out of love or even affection for people but simply so that they will leave him alone. This is first highlighted by the lie which he tells to the soldier on the bus to Marengo "just so I wouldn't have to say anything else" (4). Later, when being interrogated by the examining magistrate, Meursault will admit, almost with pride, that "always, whenever I want to get rid of someone I'm not really listening to, I made it appear as if I agreed" (69). Camus clearly presents this approach to living as self-destructive: Meursault lacks self-determination and this makes him vulnerable to people who know what they want.

Since some critics are often rather coy in describing Raymond Sintès, it is important to establish immediately that the man is a pimp. He has been trying to turn the girl he calls his "mistress" (29) into his whore by setting her up in a room and giving her "just enough to live on"; the "work" which he expects her to do, but which she refuses to do, is turning tricks, that is, prostituting herself (30). Having got that clear, the reader is in a better position to note that Sintès describes his relationship with his mistress in a way which is designed to make himself appear as a victim of her unreasonableness: he pays for her room, her food, and her clothes, and she, in return, unreasonably refuses to "'work'" (useful euphemism!) even half-days in order to help Sintès out with his expenses; she is unfaithful to him with a man who buys her two bracelets, for which Sintès beats her, something which he has never done before. The degree to which Meursault accepts Sintès' version as factual is emphasized by the words which he uses to describe the narrative, "he said ... told me ... continued ... explained ... went on ... pointed out" (29-31). These impersonal verbs, which stress the reasonableness of what Sintès is saying, are curiously at odds with the violence and emotion in the story itself, "He'd beaten her until she bled" (31), yet Meursault is oblivious to the contrast. Sintès' account reaches a pinnacle of self-contradiction with his claim that he had never "beaten" his mistress before; he had merely "smack[ed] her around a little, but nice-like" (31). The reader recoils from the artificial and dishonest distinction between beating and smacking around and finds comical the oxymoron describing someone being nicely smacked around. Camus emphasizes Meursault's passivity when he says that he "just listened," and so manipulates the reader into taking a moral position which Meursault so noticeably fails to do (31).

Just as Meursault can find no motivation to initiate action (Sundays being the most obvious example), he can find no motivation to avoid taking actions suggested by others even when they are plainly not in his own interest. Unlike his neighbors, who take a moral position on Sintès because of his criminality, Meursault, who is as unable to take a moral position on Sintès beating a woman as he is on Salamano beating his dog, makes the mistake of once again finding what Sintès "has to say interesting" (28). He uses exactly that word to describe his reaction to Sintès' account of his conflict with the Arab woman and her brother, "I said I didn't think anything but that it was interesting" (28). When he says that he does not "think," Meursault means that he makes no moral judgment on the issues raised by the story; rather he approaches it as a logical problem which he "understood" (32). The woman "seemed" (that word again!) guilty of cheating Sintès because it does not occur to Meursault to question the veracity of the narrative he has heard, and therefore he understands Sintès' "wanting to punish her" in the same way that he understood his boss's resentment at having to grant Meursault a four-day weekend (32). The prosecutor at his trial will describe Meursault as "a monster, a man without morals," but Meursault's reply, if he were a philosopher (which he is not), would be to question the basis upon which society establishes the validity of moral judgments (92).

Writing the Letter for Sintès

With the exception of shooting the Arab, writing the letter which will lure the woman into a trap is the most criminal and immoral action that Meursault performs in the novel. He knowingly enters a brutal conspiracy which is both sexist and racist. Sintès' plan is to lure the woman back so that he can make love to her because, as he tells Meursault, he "'still had sexual feelings for her,'" then to spit in her face at the moment before orgasm because he feels that "'she still hasn't gotten what she has coming'" (31). Meursault has no emotional or moral reaction to this self-evidently horrible plan; he evaluates it on a purely practical level and concludes, "Yes, that would punish her, I thought" completely ignoring the weakness of Sintès' case that the woman has been unfaithful to him, or the question of whether she has already been punished enough (32). McCarthy calls this a "puzzling episode" (28). It certainly is to anyone who thinks that Meursault is being presented at this point as the hero (rather than the protagonist) of the novel - the one honest man in Algiers. This is not, however, true. Meursault's consciousness evolves during the narrative. At this point, as McCarthy correctly explains, Meursault's inability to make moral distinctions leads him into an "episode … [which] contains the fewest elements of protest and the highest degree of alienation" (37).

When it comes to writing the letter, Meursault loses himself in the sensual experience of the activity of writing. Just as in the presence of his mother's coffin his attention was on the physical features of the room containing the coffin rather than on death, all of his attention is now focused on the textures, the colors and the shapes associated with writing, "He carefully wiped the oilcloth covering the table … he took out a sheet of paper, a yellow envelope, a small red pen box, and a square bottle with purple ink in it" (32). Having no moral values and no personal motivation, Meursault becomes a willing instrument in a criminal plot, "I tried my best to please Raymond because I didn't have any reason not to please him" (32). The reader might normally see this as a failure of intelligence or of imagination, but it is neither: it is a conviction that nothing matters, that one decision is the same as another. In a sentence which foreshadows Meursault's agreement to marry Marie, he accepts Sintès' judgment that he is a pal because, "I didn't mind being his pal, and he seemed set on it" (33) (Compare, "I said it didn't make any difference to me, and that we could if she wanted to" [41]). The reader, however, can see that Meursault's acquiescence to each proposal will place him in relationships which will erode his independence in ways which will make a radical difference to him.

Ironically, the evening ends with Meursault's illusion that these two men, so completely different in their view of life and how to live it, "understand each other" (33). Meursault comments on how late it is and remarks that "Raymond thought so too"; Sintès "remarked how quickly the time passed, and in a way it was true"; and in reference to his mother's death Raymond comments that "it was one of those things that was bound to happen sooner or later," and Meursault comments, "I thought so too" (33). The first two examples of agreement appear, of course, trivial, but since they are about the passage of time they lead directly to the third example which shows precisely the error Meursault is making: both men are aware that their time on earth is limited, neither appears to have any believe in life after death, and each believes that because of this the morality which society imposes through its laws has no validity. However, Meursault's reaction to this truth is amoral, whilst Sintès' reaction is immoral: Sintès' nihilism justifies a life of criminality which is designed to validate his existence by the exertion of his power over others, whilst Meursault's instinctive understanding of the absurdity of life empties life of all moral and emotional meaning. Thus, Meursault's action in writing the letter is passive, whilst Sintès' is proactive – not that that makes it any the less shocking.

Ironically, the last thing Meursault hears that night is "in old Salamano's room, the dog whimpering softly" which is Camus' way of alerting the reader to the parallel between the brutality of Salamano and Sintès and of showing how Meursault has gone from ignoring brutality to being complicit in it (33).

Meursault ends his account of this episode with a very significant statement, "All I could hear was the blood pounding in my ears" (33) which almost exactly parallels his comment as he was approaching Maman's grave-side, "I could feel the blood pounding in my temples" (17). Meursault will make an identical observation shortly before he shoots the Arab on the beach, "my forehead especially was hurting me, all the veins in it throbbing under the skin" (58-9). Like the hot sun, the rushing blood is a sign of the social pressure which Meursault feels himself to be under at these points. The comments also indicate how completely egotistical Meursault is: everything literally begins and ends with him.

Summary:

Faced with the cruel mathematics of mortality, length of life is of no importance.

Because of death, nothing in life matters and one choice is as good as another.

Strong-willed people live their lives in defiance of these two truths.

Meursault is vulnerable to such people.

Convinced that there are not transcendent values, Meursault lives in a valueless world.

In terms of how he lives his life, this chapter probably shows the worse aspects of Meursault.

PART ONE Chapter 4: Social Constraints

First we form habits, then they form us. (Rob Gilbert)

Consider the following:

1. What expression does Meursault use twice to describe his attraction to Marie? What does it tell you about him?

2. "A minute later she asked me if I loved her. I told her it didn't mean anything but that I didn't think so" (35). Is Meursault's reaction to Marie's question honest or insensitive? Perhaps you feel it is both?

3. Contrast the reactions of Meursault and Marie to the incident involving Raymond, the woman and the policeman. How is Meursault's reaction to the beaten woman similar to his reaction to Marie's question?

4. Comment on the unconscious irony of Meursault's conclusion, "I found him very friendly with me and I thought it was a nice moment" (38).

5. What Meursault hears Mr. Salamano crying he comments, "For some reason I thought of Maman" (39). Explain what is it that he is failing to understand.

6. What is significant about Meursault's eating and sleeping in this chapter?

Of Sex and Love:

The years which Camus spent working towards and then drafting the novel which became *The Stranger* were punctuated by marriage (to Simone Hié in 1934) and divorce, a series of love affairs (with, amongst others, Lucette Meurer and Yvonne Ducailar), and a second marriage (to Francine Faure in 1940). Camus was a promiscuous adulterer who was apparently incapable of remaining faithful to one woman. Olivier Todd records Camus' thoughts on love in his *Noces*; they help us to understand Meursault's view of love:

> Books and legends are responsible for a collective view of seeing that makes us call love that which ties us to certain people … All I know about love is a mix of desire, tenderness, and intelligence that links me to one such person, and this combination is not the same for everyone, so I cannot describe every experience with the same term, nor need I use the same gestures with everyone.(Quoted in Todd 97)

One can see here that Camus' objection to the term "love" is that it is a meaningless generalization – a kind of catch-all term which does not describe accurately the feelings of one individual for another individual since these feelings are not capable of being generalized; they are unique in every case. Obviously, Camus (a man given to self-examination) is more conscious of his reasons for rejecting the term "love" than is his protagonist Meursault, but each ultimately finds it meaningless for the same reasons.

The Developing Relationship of Meursault and Marie

The physical nature of Meursault's relationship with Marie is stressed by his repeated use of the phrase, "I wanted her" which conveys the strength of his sexual attraction to her (34, 35). The first weeks of their affair are something of an idyll: Marie's physical attractions appear to blend perfectly (harmoniously) with the sensual pleasures of Algiers in the summer. Meursault describes Marie in a way which stresses bright, lively colors and yielding textures, "in that pretty red-and-white striped dress and leather sandals … the shape of her firm breasts … her tan made her face look like a flower" (34). The final simile presents Marie as part of the natural world an identification which will be developed further in the narrative.

Given the significance of the sun and heat later in the novel, it is significant that Meursault describes his experience at the beach with Marie by stressing the pleasing sensation of warmth from the sun, "The four o'clock sun wasn't too hot," from the sea, "the water was warm, with slow, gently lapping waves" (34), and, in contrast, the cooling effect of Marie, "her tongue cooled my lips" (35). Marie teaches him a game which involves taking foam into the mouth and then turning on one's back to spout it out into the air. This game seems to symbolize the heightened sensual pleasure which Marie has brought into his life. His description is full of words which emphasize the game's stimulating effect on touch and taste, "delicate … warm spray … stinging … salty bitterness … pressed herself against me … we tumbled" (34-5). The complete harmony which Meursault feels at this point between the life he is leading and the physical world reaches its apotheosis in the image which he uses to describe himself and Marie back in his apartment after having made love, "the summer night air flowing over our brown bodies felt good" (35). In this image, sky and sea seem to be one, and the tanned bodies of the lovers seem to unite them with the earth; if it is going too far to say that the air seems to be administering a kind of benediction on the couple (and I am not sure that it *is* going too far), then at least we can say that Meursault perceives the evening air as benevolent. In other words, in his happiness, Meursault is once again making the mistake of anthropomorphizing natural phenomena.

What is for Meursault the perfect relationship is, however, just about to be shattered by Marie. This is foreshadowed when Meursault hears "a woman's voice in Raymond's room" and Salamano swearing at his dog on the stairs. These sounds serve to remind the reader that Meursault has involved himself in a cruel, misogynistic scheme of revenge. Ironically, at the very moment when Meursault is thinking exclusively of sex with Marie, "I wanted her again" (35), she asks him if he loves her, a question which reveals that Marie's physical attraction to Meursault has developed into a deeper sentimental and emotional attachment. Meursault gives a precisely honest answer, "I told her that it didn't mean anything, but that I didn't think so. She looked sad. But as we were fixing lunch, and for no apparent reason, she laughed in such a way that I kissed her" (35).

Since Meursault does not know what love is, he can only give an opinion that what he is feeling for Marie is not what society seems to mean when it uses the word "love." (The reader sees that Meursault's unwillingness or inability to admit to loving Marie parallels his unwillingness or inability to grieve for his mother.) He records her look of sadness without comment. Of course, he understands from experience that people appear to be sad when others disagree with them, but he does not understand the emotion of sadness because (like love) he has never personally experienced it. Meursault is completely at a loss to explain Marie's laugh because it is clearly inconsistent with her previous sadness – once again he reveals the difficulty he has in reading people. There are a number of occasions in the novel where Camus relies on the reader's ability to interpret the reactions of characters when Meursault is unable to do so, and this is one of them. It is clear that Marie's laugh is her way of minimizing the negative response she has just received; she literally laughs it off, explaining it in terms of Meursault's peculiarity, of that difference from the other men who she has known which is a large part of what makes him attractive to her. Her reaction tells the reader that Marie is looking for more than physical satisfaction in her relationship with Meursault and that she is unlikely to be deflected by one negative answer. This being so, the idyll is about to end.

Meursault and Raymond Sintès

Another relationship is also leading independently to the destruction of Meursault's idyll: his involvement with Sintès' plan for revenge against the Arab woman. At this point in the narrative, the plot literally breaks into the quiet of Meursault's apartment in the form Sintès' angry accusations and the cries of the woman being beaten. Meursault's word-selection leaves the reader in no doubt as to the violence of

Sintès' attack, "fight … shrill voice … thuds … screamed … terrifying … shrieking … hitting … crying … hit" (35-6). Marie's reaction is contrasted with that of Meursault. As a woman, Marie empathizes with the victim even though she has never met her and even though she is an Arab, but Meursault (whose reaction is consistent with his attitude to Salamano beating his dog) remains noncommittal and uninvolved, "Marie said it was terrible and I didn't say anything" (36). The use of the conjunction "and" rather than the more obvious 'but' is significant here since it illustrates Meursault's inability to make causal links when these are based on positive emotion such as sympathy and pity. Marie's reaction is moral outrage, and she instinctively appeals to an external moral authority to restore order, "She asked me to go find a policeman, but I told her I didn't like cops" (36). Here Meursault does use the conjunction "but" because he finds his dislike of the police to be reasonable. Meursault has no emotional reaction to the sounds of violence, and he has no respect for civil authority, so he places his own concerns above those of the victim and even of Marie just as he did when he told Marie that he did not love her. In his massive egotism, he can empathize with neither.

Camus uses Sintès' encounter with the policeman to question the validity of the civil authorities. Despite (perhaps even because of) Meursault's noncommittal account of Sintès' slapping of his mistress, the reader perceives the act as unjust and immoral. When the cop slaps Raymond because he is being insolent, the reader perceives both slaps to be identical: in each case, the person in a position of power uses that power to coerce the weaker person. The reader may enjoy the irony of the bully Sintès being bullied and being so afraid that he is literally shaking as he stands in front of the policeman, but the incident has the effect of making the two protagonists appear to be more similar than dissimilar. In this way, Camus implicitly challenges the society's claim to represent a valid moral order.

Meursault and Sintès appear to have the same attitudes to the police, "[t]he two share a dislike for the representatives of authority" (McCarthy 40). However, their dislike has a very different basis. For the criminal Sintès, the police are rivals: he does not question their authority; he simply pits it against his own strong will. However, Meursault is not a habitual criminal even though Sintès has dragged him into criminal activity. The reader can see what Meursault himself, an unaware man, cannot: his objection to the police is the objection of the dissenter although at present Meursault is unable to express his feelings in the language of dissent. In Part Two, Meursault will come to understand that he "didn't like cops" because he does not accept the legitimacy of the State's claim to decide and to enforce the moral law "in the name of some vague notion called the French (or German, or Chinese) people" (109). He will learn the language of dissent.

The conclusion of the incident is almost comic. Once the policeman has taken Sintès away, Meursault and Marie finish getting lunch ready, but when it comes to eating Marie has no appetite whilst Meursault eats heartily, "she wasn't hungry; I ate almost everything" (37). Notice that once again that Meursault avoids the obvious conjunction 'but,' instead using a semi-colon to juxtapose the two statements without causally linking them. Meursault amazingly makes no connection between the emotional upset caused to Marie by the incident which she has witnessed and her loss of appetite because he suffers no such reaction. When Marie leaves, Meursault does what he often does when faced by demanding social situations: he sleeps.

The Continued Manipulation of Meursault

When Sintès returns to Meursault's apartment, the narrative makes it clear how easily he is able to manipulate Meursault who is vulnerable precisely because he makes no moral judgment on the beating of the girl. Meursault tells Sintès, "it seemed to me that she'd gotten her punishment now and that he ought to be happy," and records that "[h]e thought so too" (37). What is significant here is that, in order to foster the sense of unity between Meursault and himself, Sintès is lying since during his argument with the policemen he told the girl, "'You just wait, sweetheart – we're not through yet'" (36). However, it is important to his manipulation of Meursault that Sintès appears to be in control of the situation. This is why he makes sure that he has lost no face in Meursault's eyes by not hitting the policeman, and, having been assured that Meursault "wasn't expecting anything," he "seemed pretty happy" (37). Reassured that Meursault still regards him as a "pal," Sintès makes a statement which changes their relationship as fundamentally as Marie's earlier question changes theirs, "He told me that I'd have to act as a witness for him" (37). Sintès' use of an imperative alerts the reader to the fact that Meursault has just lost his independence and freedom of action: he has to testify precisely because he is Sintès' "pal"; this relationship, like his relationship with Marie, now comes with strings attached.

Meursault is perfectly willing to act as a witness provided Sintès tells him what to say, in the same way that he will later be perfectly willing to marry Marie and for the same reason. He tells Sintès, "It didn't matter to me" (37). (Compare, "I explained to her that it didn't really matter and that if she wanted to, we could get married" [41].) Lacking self-motivation, and convinced that one choice is as good as another, Meursault is exceptionally vulnerable to strong-willed people who know what they want. Having achieved his objective, Sintès binds Meursault closer to him by playing on their status as "pals." There is more male bonding: they drink (Sintès pays), shoot pool (Sintès lets Meursault almost win), and Sintès suggests visiting a whorehouse.

As they walk home, Sintès shares his satisfaction with the way their plan has worked out because "the woman [got] what she deserved," and Meursault comments, "I found him very friendly with me and I thought it was a nice moment" (38). Camus uses comic irony here to expose Meursault's naiveté. Not only is he unaware of the extent to which he is being played by a criminal, but he has no awareness that the word "nice" is totally inappropriate when discussing beating up a woman. Here, if nowhere else in the novel, one is rather tempted to agree with Colin Wilson's assessment (in *The Outsider*) that "the hero of [*The Stranger*] is basically a brainless idiot" (quoted in Scherr 150). Camus himself was saying the same thing, though in rather less provocative language, when he explained Meursault's passivity in this way, "[he is] a negative character insofar as he seems deprived of subjectivity" (quoted in Gay-Crosier 65).

Meursault and Salamano

In a chapter which focuses on relationships, it is fitting that Meursault's last encounter brings him into contact with the end of Salamano's relationship with his dog. Camus presents the loss of the dog as a rather cruel joke: Salamano is watching "'The King of the Escape Artists'" when it slips its collar and escapes! The dog has effectively died, and the initial description of Salamano "looking all over the place ... peering into the darkness ... searching the street again with his little red eyes" deliberately parallels the description of the crying and frustrated Perez desperately, and unsuccessfully, trying to keep up with the procession to the grave-side. Both old men symbolize man's powerlessness in the face of loss and death.

Salamano keeps up the fiction that he hates the dog in order to save face. It becomes clear, however, that he desperately needs the companionship of the dog in order to go on with his life. This is the significance of his desperate need to be reassured that the authorities will not "take him away" (39). His concern, however, is not for the dog but for himself. He pathetically asks, "'They're not going to take him away from me, are they, Monsieur Meursault? They'll give him back to me. Otherwise, what's going to happen to me?'" (39). The dog is Salamano's essential defense against the terrifying truth of his mortality.

Evidently, Camus intends the reader to draw parallels between Salamano's relationship with his dog and Meursault's relationship with his mother. Salamano's indifference to his dog, unlike Meursault's inability to grieve for his mother, is a mere façade. Alone in his room, Meursault hears him "pacing back and forth," then hears a "peculiar little noise coming through the partition" and realizes that Salamano is crying (39) which recalls the "[b]ig tears of frustration and exhaustion" which Meursault noted running down Perez's cheeks (18). Salamano is showing the grief for the loss of his dog which Meursault never showed for Maman, and this fact brings Meursault face-to-face with the emptiness of his life. At some level, but not at the conscious level, he makes the connection, "For some reason, I thought of Maman" (39). Meursault's inability to make connections is further stressed when he says without explanation, "I wasn't hungry, and I went to bed without any dinner" (39). The reader knows that Meursault has no appetite for the same reasons that Marie had no appetite for lunch – he is too upset, not for the death of his mother, but for the paucity of the life which he is living which that death has revealed. Typically, he seeks escape from the pressures which have built on him in this chapter in sleep.

Summary:

Meursault's relationship with Marie appears to combine maximum sensual gratification with zero emotional attachment, leading him to feel that he is living in harmony with the physical world.

Marie's love for Meursault threatens to change completely the nature of their relationship.

Being a "pal" carries obligations the nature of which Meursault fails to understand.

Meursault's relationships with Marie and Sintès threaten to destroy the independence from society which is the basis of his life as a stranger.

Salamano's relationship with his dog is a habit which makes it easier for him to avoid thinking about death.

PART ONE Chapter 5: Life-changing Decisions

> A man without ethics is a wild beast loosed upon this world. (Albert Camus)

Consider the following:

1. Why do you think that Meursault has no desire to live in Paris? What does the boss find unsatisfactory about Meursault's reaction to his offer? (Comment on Meursault's expression, "He looked upset" [41].)

2. "Then she pointed out that marriage was a serious thing. I said, 'No'" (42). Explain why Marie and Meursault have such a different view of marriage. Why does Marie decide that she wants to marry Meursault despite this difference of opinion?

3. What is significant about Meursault's reaction to the "strange little woman" at Celeste's (43)? [Note that this character will reappear later to watch Meursault's trial and appear to judge him.]

4. Comment on the following aspects of Meursault's dialogue with Salamano:

a) the way in which Salamano tries to impose some meaning on Meursault's life and actions;

b) the theme of the inevitability of decay and death;

c) Meursault's reaction on learning that some people had been critical of his decision to put his mother in a home.

5. Without his narrator being aware of it, Camus has set up a conflict that will have a catastrophic impact on Meursault's life. Trace the way in which this has been developed in the novel.

Unexpected Consequences

The chapter opens with a clear indication that Meursault's involvement with Sintès will continue to impact his life. In what is to the reader (but not to Meursault) merely a gambit designed to cement their status as "pals," Sintès calls Meursault at the office to invite him to a friend's beach house on Sunday. Initially, Meursault declines the invitation citing a prior arrangement to "spend the day with a girlfriend" (40). Sintès, however, extends the invitation to the girlfriend and says how pleased his friend's wife will be "not to be alone with a bunch of men," and by doing so he unknowingly unites the two sets of social obligation into which Meursault is being drawn (40). As we shall see, the time spent at the beach house will show Meursault how marriage to Marie would change his life in ways that he would find intolerable. More ominously, the call from Sintès makes it clear that the incident with the Arab woman has resulted in a feud with her brother and his friends that clearly also has racial overtones. Sintès asks Meursault to keep a lookout for the brother around their apartment building, and he agrees, "I said I would" without showing any understanding of the danger into which he is getting himself (40).

The Chance to Take Control of One's Future

In this chapter, Meursault is presented with two opportunities to change his life: his boss offers him a promotion, and Marie suggests that they should get married. Meursault rejects one proposal and accepts the other but his reason is the same in each case: he is not convinced that either choice will change his life in any significant way. Meursault lacks the self-awareness fully to understand the basis of his own negativity, but to the reader it clearly springs from his conviction of the meaninglessness of all human endeavors in the face of death. The boss appears to have mistaken Meursault's hard work for youthful drive and ambition in much the same way that Marie has mistaken his being sexually attracted to her for love. Both are disappointed when

Meursault's response shows them the mistake they have made, but he is limited to recording their appearance of sorrow because he has no understanding of the emotional depth of their disappointment. Significantly, Meursault uses virtually the same words to record his observations: the boss "looked upset" at his lack of enthusiasm for the promotion (43) just as Marie earlier "looked sad" (35) when he told her that he did not think that he loved her.

An Opportunity to Change his Career:

Significantly, Meursault's first reaction when his boss sends for him is to feel annoyed because he is convinced that his boss is going to complain about his using the office phone to discuss his personal life. Despite what Camus himself wrote, in Part One Meursault tries very hard to 'play the game' by society's rules and gets frustrated by his failures. Here, as so often, Meursault mistakenly projects his internal feelings of guilt onto another person, and therefore he is relieved, and perhaps a little flattered, when the boss says that he wants to "talk" to him (40) and get his "opinion" (41). In considering his boss's offer, Meursault is forced to reflect on his reasons for not wishing to accept, and this provides the reader with important insight into his view of life. Meursault believes that "people never change their lives, that in any case one life was as good as another," and this being so he is does not want to put up with the practical disruption to his existence which moving to Paris would inevitably cause (41). Although he has not thought it through, Meursault seems to be making two claims here: firstly, people never change their lives because people never change their consciousness (Meursault in Paris will still be Meursault, and so nothing will have changed); and, secondly, since values are meaningless abstractions there is no measure by which to judge the quality or validity of one way of living over another.

There is a hint as to the origins of Meursault's cynical view of life – the only one given in the entire novel. When he was a student, Meursault recollects, he "had ambitions … But when I had to give up my studies I learned quickly that none of it really mattered" (41). Although it is not explicitly stated, the clue to Meursault's indifference is that he found that he was as content with his life after having been forced to give up his dreams as he was when he was pursuing those dreams, or more accurately that he "wasn't unhappy" with his life after he gave up his ambitions (41). (Camus certainly drew here on his own experience. Having obtained his Diploma of Advanced Studies in May 1936, he planned to pursue his studies at post-graduate level but was prevented from doing so by his tuberculosis.)

Later, Meursault will record that his mother taught him to adapt to his life rather than to seek to change his life, "it was one of Maman's ideas, and she often repeated it, that after a while you could get used to anything" (77). Meursault thus got into the habit of accepting the disappointment of his ambitions so completely that he lost any motivation to take control of his life. It is significant, however, that Meursault can only use negative terms to describe his current way of life: he does not say that his life is happy, he says that it is not "unhappy"; he does not say that he is satisfied by the life he is living, he says that he is not "dissatisfied … at all" (41). Following his final epiphany, he will have learned that life can be defined in positive terms, but that is far into the future.

An Opportunity to Change his Personal Life:

The connective that Meursault uses in his account of his conversation with Marie that evening is "Then" – the word is used five times on page forty-two. It is as though Meursault can find no way of linking the various things that happen between him and Marie other than chronologically. Significantly, in his telephone conversation with Raymond at the start of this chapter, Meursault refers to Marie as "a girlfriend," the indefinite article indicating that he attributes no special significance to his relationship with her (40). When Marie suggests marriage, Meursault's reaction is expressed in exactly the same terms as was his reaction to his boss's proposal; he tells Marie "it didn't make any difference to me,"

84

which echoes his response to his boss who he tells "it was all the same to me" (41). In both cases, Meursault, having no motivation of his own, seems open to taking a course of action simply because someone else strongly wants him to take it. In the case of his boss, he originally says "yes" to the proposal (41), and in response to Marie he is even more amenable, "she was the one who was doing the asking and all I was saying was yes" (41-2). Meursault is so vulnerable to the stronger will of Marie precisely because he cannot conceive that married life will be fundamentally different from life with Marie as his mistress - after all Meursault will still be Meursault. This explains the difference between Marie, who understands that marriage is a life-changing event, a "big thing," and Meursault who does not (42).

It is perhaps easier to understand Meursault's thinking in this episode than it is to understand Marie's continuing desire to marry him. This is largely because the reader is reliant on Meursault's observations of Marie's reaction, and, as we have seen, Meursault is an unreliable observer of others because of his limited understanding of what motivates other people. After Meursault has said that he does not regard getting married as serious, there is a pause in the conversation which Meursault records without any interpretation. When Marie next asks if he would have agreed to marry another woman, he presents the question in a way which shows that he does not regard it as important, "She just wanted to know if I would have accepted the same proposal from another woman, with whom I was involved in the same way" (42). The word "just" indicates that to Meursault this is an easy question to answer, and his casual answer, "I said, 'Sure,'" is both honest and heartless (43). The next thing that he records is Marie wondering aloud if she really loves him; Meursault appears to have no idea why she says this or why she is then once again silent for a moment. To the reader, it is clear that Marie's actions are designed manipulate Meursault, to get some response from him, but since he does not understand this he offers no response.

Why, then, does Marie still say that she loves and wants to marry him? The clue is in her use of the word "peculiar" to describe Meursault (42). He is different from any man she has known, more honest and less conventional, and that if what attracts her. Two examples of this Meursault's peculiarity occur on their walk through Algiers that evening. Firstly, Meursault comments of the beauty of the other women he sees without any thought that this might offend his girlfriend, "The women were beautiful, and I asked Marie if she'd noticed. She said yes and that she understood what I meant" (42). Marie responds positively to Meursault's unconventional honesty because she understands that the women represent no threat to her since Meursault has just agreed to marry her. Secondly he shows no curiosity, and voices no objection, when Marie tells him that she "had something to do" (42). Initially, Marie is surprised by his reaction and asks him, "'Don't you want to know what I have to do?'" (42). Meursault's initial reaction, typically, is that his lack of interest has caused him to commit a social faux pas, and he comments, "she seemed to be scolding me" (42). Far from scolding him for not wanting to know what it is that she has to do, Marie is delighted by this aspect of his peculiarity: Meursault is not a possessive lover, and Marie finds this refreshing and unusual, "she laughed again and she moved towards me with her whole body to offer me her lips" (42-3).

The two opportunities which Meursault is offered to take control of the direction of his life are linked when, having agreed to marry Marie, he tells her of the boss's offer. Immediately she puts pressure on him to accept, "she said she'd love to see Paris" (42). Meursault's reaction is immediately negative. He associates Paris with the opposite of the sensual life which is represented by Algeria, "I told her that I'd lived there once and she asked what it was like. I said, 'It's dirty. Lots of pigeons and dark courtyards. Everybody's pale'" (42). For Meursault, whose life revolves around sensual gratification, Paris holds no attraction, but he now finds himself in a position where two strong-willed people, his boss and Marie, want him to go there.

The Proactive Life

Whilst having dinner at Celeste's, Meursault becomes fascinated by a "strange little woman" with "robotlike movements" who sits at his table (43). He observes her closely and even follows her for a while. She is never still, and the strong verbs used to describe her actions suggest control: she "studied the menu feverishly … ordered her whole meal all at once … added up the bill in advance … took the exact amount, plus tip, out of a vest pocket" (43). In between courses, she plans her radio listening for the week. Superficially, the woman seems to be like Meursault since both live their lives based upon routine, yet the difference is that the robot-woman plans her routine whereas Meursault simply adapts to the routine of the office. Meursault finds the woman "peculiar" without actually saying (perhaps without knowing) why (44). It is ironic that he uses exactly the same word to describe this woman as Marie uses to describe him: Marie recognizes that Meursault is radically different from herself just as Meursault realizes that the little woman is radically different from him. In fact, the woman is Meursault's exact opposite: proactive rather than reactive. She "meticulously" plans every aspect of her life in advance from her dinner bill to her radio listening. Unlike Meursault, she takes control of her life with great energy and confidence "making her way with incredible speed and assurance, never once swerving or looking around" (43). What fascinates Meursault (although he is not able to articulate this) is that this woman lives her life as though she is not bounded by mortality. The comic absurdity of checking off radio programs is that one might not be around to hear them. Meursault is surrounded in the novel by people who live their lives with "incredible speed and assurance" (43) but who do not live authentic lives because they do not really have the control over their lives which they assume that they have. These people, like the robot woman, are living life in denial, living absurd lives without being aware of the absurdity of life. This, of course, explains why these are the people who will return at his trial to condemn Meursault.

Living as a Habit

Meursault's meeting with Salamano allows Camus to examine once again the inadequacies of both the planned life and the adaptive life. Like Meursault, Salamano had ambitions plans for his life when he was young, and like Meursault these plans came to nothing, "When he was young he'd wanted to go into the theater … But he's ended up working on the railways, and he didn't regret it" (44). (Compare Meursault's comment that "when I had to give up my studies I learned very quickly that none of it really mattered" [41].) In fact, Salamano's life seems to exemplify Meursault's view that one life is much the same as another. Salamano tells the story of the different stages of his life illustrating how, at each stage, he attempted to adapt. He gave up his acting ambition, but he found compensation in the fact that the railways provide a small pension; he was not happy with his wife, but "he'd pretty much gotten used to her"; he was "lonely" when his wife died, but he solved that problem by getting "used to" a dog (44). Indeed, perhaps because he comes from the same generation, Salamano's life seems to embody Maman's maxim that "after a while you can get used to anything" (77). It is important to note, however, that Meursault's mother did not hold this view in the final years and months of her life – a fact which becomes clear to the reader only at the end of the novel.

Salamano is in many ways similar to that other old man Perez in that both fail to live authentically: the essential difference is that whilst Perez strives to control his life (symbolically by trying to keep up with the hearse), Salamano simply tries to accommodate himself to life. One is proactive and the other reactive, but it makes no difference; together they exemplify the truth of the Nurse's statement that, "'If you go slowly, you risk getting sunstroke. But if you go too fast, you work up a sweat and then catch a chill inside the church'" (17). That there is no way out of mortality is illustrated by the accelerated aging process which is killing Salamando's dog. When the dog begins to suffer from skin disease, Salamano does what he has done throughout his life: her tries to make the best of it. Night and morning, he rubs ointment into the dog's skin, but he knows that what he is doing is useless because the dog's disease is mortality, "according to him [Salamano], the dog's real sickness was old age, and there's no cure for old age" (45). The irony is that with the loss of his dog Salamano is forced to admit the very thing that Meursault has denied throughout the chapter, "His life had changed now and he wasn't sure what he was going to do" (emphasis added 45-6). Salamano has run out of coping strategies. Getting used to the disappointments of life is no more valid than vainly trying to control life, and in this way his story is as much a warning to Meursault as are the stories of Perez and the little robot-woman.

The Expectations of Society

The conversation with Salamano also brings home to Meursault once again the expectations which society has of him. Salamano transitions from talking about his dog to discussing Meursault's mother:

> He told me that Maman was very fond of his dog. He called her 'you poor mother.' He said he supposed I must be very sad since Maman died, and I didn't say anything. Then he said, very quickly and with an embarrassed look, that he realized that some people in the neighborhood thought badly of me for having sent Maman to the home, but he knew me and he knew I loved her very much. (45)

This is both offensive and threatening to Meursault on many levels. Firstly, Salamano calls Maman "'your poor mother'" and repeats society's expectation that a son "must be very sad" at his mother's death (45). Meursault says nothing because he has nothing to say: Maman had not been part of his life for several years, and he does not miss her because he has got used to her not being there. Secondly, Meursault learns for the first time that opinion in the neighborhood is against him for having "sent" his mother to the home (45). Always sensitive to the charge of having offended against the expectations of society, Meursault finds it necessary to defend himself against this charge explaining to Salamano that moving Maman to the home "seemed like the natural thing since I didn't have enough money to have Maman cared for" (45). Clearly, emotions had no part in the decision, which leads to Salamano's final offense, the assertion that, despite all appearances to the contrary, he "knew" that Meursault loved his mother "very much" (45). This reminds us of Marie's decision to marry Meursault even after he tells her that he has no wish to marry and that he does not love her. It seems that society is not prepared to allow Meursault to go through the motions of conforming: he must have feelings, and for their own satisfaction people assume that, despite any appearance to the contrary, Meursault does have feelings which he just finds it difficult to express. Both Marie and Salamano are interpreting and molding Meursault in a way that validates the rational order that each needs to find in the world.

Summary:

Meursault's involvement with Sintès drags him into a family feud which has racial overtones.

The boss's offer of a promotion threatens to disrupt Meursault's Algerian life-style.

Marie's proposal threatens to take away his independence.

The robot-woman and Salamano each epitomize unsatisfactory and inauthentic responses to human mortality.

Salamano exerts upon Meursault the pressures of social expectations to which he is expected to conform.

PART ONE Chapter 6: Confronting Mortality

> To be, or not to be: that is the question:
> Whether 'tis nobler in the mind to suffer
> The slings and arrows of outrageous fortune,
> Or to take arms against a sea of troubles,
> And by opposing end them...
> (William Shakespeare *Hamlet* 3.1)

Consider the following:

1. Comment on the simile "the day, already bright with sun, hit me like a slap in the face" (47). How does it foreshadow the dramatic events that will happen at the beach?

2. In what ways is Meursault's comment on Raymond's white hairy arms, "I found it a little repulsive" typical of him (47-8)? (Compare it with his complaint about towels in the washroom at work and contrast it with his failure to make any judgment about Raymond's immorality.)

3. How does Camus make the encounter with the Arabs by the tobacconist's shop ominous?

4. How does Meursault's description of his first visit to the beach and of swimming with Marie emphasize the way in which he enjoys the natural environment?

5. How does Meursault's description of the natural environment (particularly the sun and the sand) differ when he gives an account of walking on the beach after lunch? (Show how Camus' use of language becomes increasingly ornate, featuring such rhetorical devices as personification and metaphor, and contrasting strongly with the spare, simple descriptions that Meursault usually offers.)

6. What is typical about Meursault's role in the first violent encounter with the two Arabs and his reaction to the women when the men have returned to the house?

7. Meursault makes a number of judgments in this chapter. Comment on the validity of the following:

a) "It was then that I realized that you could either shoot or not shoot" (56);

b) "But the heat was so intense that it was just as bad standing still … To stay or go, it amounted to the same thing … I turned back toward the beach …" (57);

c) "As far as I was concerned, the whole thing was over, and I'd gone there without even thinking about it" (58).

8. Why does Meursault go to the beach the third time?

Structure of *The Stranger*

Parts One and Two of the novel each end structurally in the same way: there is an epiphany and a physical conflict. In Part One, Meursault has a moment of partial insight as he is walking back to the beach house following the second of three confrontations with the Arabs. This is significant because, for the first time in the novel, Meursault consciously reflects upon the human condition even though he comes to erroneous conclusions. Meursault's new understanding of human freedom has to two significant consequences. Firstly, he will never again feel the need to conform to society; from this point on in the novel, he will begin to develop into a conscious rebel against authority and will increasingly use the language of descent. Secondly, he will shoot an Arab who represents no threat to himself. Since these consequences are at the heart of the novel's meaning, they will require detailed analysis.

The Essential Problem of Interpretation

McCarthy uses the title "An Arab is somehow murdered" for his analysis of the shooting. His interpretation centers on answering the related questions: "what is the sun and why is it so hostile to Meursault?" (45). He admits, however, that his "attempts to make sense of this hostility by using psychological and political readings … [leave] much in the chapter that cannot be explained," and places the responsibility for this on the failure of Camus' "forceful" explanation of the sun's hostility presented in "a discourse on the sun composed in lyrical language" (45) which McCarthy argues to be "unsatisfactory because it cannot be translated into the language of the rest of the book" (45-6). Of course, artistic works can be inconsistent, faulty, flawed; *The Stranger* is not artistically perfect. However, critical analysis can also be flawed. At least, McCarthy sets the criterion by which any satisfactory analysis of the shooting must be judged: it must explain the significance of the sun's hostility in a way which is consistent with the presentation of the sun in the novel as a whole. The present reading is an attempt to do this.

An Ominous Beginning

The chapter begins with negative foreshadowing. Meursault, who has a heightened awareness of sense impressions, wakes feeling "completely drained" with a "slight headache," his first cigarette "tasted bitter" (47), and he finds the black hairs on Raymond's arms "a little repulsive" (47-8). More significantly, although it is early morning and therefore objectively speaking not oppressively hot, the summer sun, from which he has so often derived pleasure, seems to be an enemy, "the day, already bright with sun, hit me like a slap in the face" (47). The description recalls the "inhuman and oppressive sun" which made Maman's funeral such an ordeal (15), a parallel which is further enforced by Marie's joking observation that Meursault has on a "'funeral face'" (47).

To understand Meursault's feeling that the sun is attacking him, it is important to remember that his perception of the sun during his walk to the funeral church was related to the strain he was feeling as a result of the emotional demands being placed upon him by the social formalities surrounding his mother's burial (15). It is the same here. Recall that in the previous chapter when Sintès telephones Meursault at work to suggest the Sunday excursion to his friend's beach house, Meursault's initial reaction is "to hang up right away" because of his boss's dislike of personal calls during working hours (40). Meursault has lost the ability to keep his working and his private lives separate. However, because Sintès goes on talking, Meursault pretends to agree with him, "I said I would" (40) - an avoidance strategy which pulls Meursault further into his relationship with Sintès and widens that relationship to include Sintès' friend Masson and his wife. Nowhere does Meursault explicitly make the connection between his perception of the sun as hostile and those times when he feels the pressures of social conformity most acutely; Camus leaves it to the reader to recognize this pattern in the narrative.

The previous night, Meursault accompanied Sintès to the police station and gave evidence that Sintès' mistress had been unfaithful to him, and, as a result, Sintès has been let off with a warning. At this point in the plot, Camus exploits the simmering hatred and lack of communication between the *pied-noir* and the native Arabs to add tension. Sintès notices the presence of a group of Arabs one of whom he identifies as the brother of the woman he beat up. What is significance about Meursault's description of the Arabs is that it illustrates his complete naiveté: it simply does not occur to him that because he "testified that the girl had cheated on Raymond," he is in as much danger from the Arabs as is Sintès (48). Thus, Meursault, having noticed that the presence of the Arabs worries Sintès, calmly explains to Marie that "they were Arabs who had it in for Raymond" (48).

It is important to acknowledge that Meursault's description of the Arabs is inherently (if not explicitly) racist. He describes them as a group rather than as a collection of individuals, and his description utilizes racist stereotyping, "They were staring at us in silence, but in that way of theirs, as if we were nothing but stones or dead trees" (emphasis added 48). Clearly this description adds to the menace posed by the Arabs, but more importantly it reveals once again the inauthenticity of Meursault's existence: he quite simply does not recognize the humanity of other people, in this case, people of a race he has been brought up to regard as inferior. It has not occurred to him that he is staring at the Arabs in exactly the same silent manner as he says they are staring at him or as he stared at the old people at Maman's vigil. The colonial situation, however, makes a significant difference. Whereas, up to this point in the novel, Meursault has always been the stranger, the individual voyeur, he is now forced to identify himself with a group because the apparent antagonism of the Arabs forces him into a them and "us" situation (48).

The Beauty of the Morning

Once the three are away from the immediate threat of the Arabs and are in the outskirts of Algiers, the mood of the narrative changes completely. Meursault, ever sensitive to his environment, notices every detail of the morning's beauty. The colors are for the most part soothing, "yellowish rocks … whitest asphodels … green or white fences," the only exception being the ominous "hard blue of the sky" (49). Everything else is subdued and calm. The sea is "motionless" and "clear … dazzling," the trawler in the distance "moving, almost imperceptibly" (49). Having apparently escaped the external pressures of the Arabs and entered an environment where he can enjoy the sensual pleasures of the day with Marie without thinking of marriage, Meursault appears to be in a place (psychologically and physically) where he can be happy.

There is, however, one image which, superficially joyful, has negative undertones. Meursault describes Marie "having fun scattering the petals [of the white asphodels], taking big swipes at them with her oilcloth bag" (49). Camus intends the reader to remember that in the Chapter 4, at a point before she talked of marriage and when their relationship seemed to be based only on mutual sensual gratification, Meursault said of Marie, "her tan made her face look like a flower" (34). The juxtaposition of these two images shows that where once Marie was perceived my Meursault to be a part of nature, she is now nature's antagonist, and her weapon is "her oilcloth bag" which contains food which Marie has packed as well as "our bathing suits and a towel" (47). In other words, the bag seems to be a symbol of domesticity, of their new-found status as an engaged couple, so it is this which has shattered the harmony between Marie and the natural world. Significantly, Meursault will later think that the Arabs managed to follow them to the beach because they noticed Marie's beach bag as they boarded the bus, a detail which unites the domestic and the criminal and racial pressures to which he feels himself to be increasingly subject.

The predominantly positive mood is continued when Meursault, Marie and Masson go down to the beach for a swim. Meursault is almost overwhelmed by the combined sensual experience of the sun, the seawater and Marie. He enjoys the contrast between the "hot" sand and the "cold" water (50); the physical "closeness … unison" which he shares when swimming with Marie (50); the "nice" experience of lying beside Masson with his head on the sand (51); the sight of Marie "glistening all over with salty water" (51); and finally the sexually stimulating feel of Marie's body, "I felt her legs wrapped around mine and I wanted her" (51). Virtually alone in the sea, Meursault's relationship with Marie can be reduced to its physical level; it is she who reminds him that he has not kissed her, and it is she who takes him back into the water. Thoughts of marriage are temporarily forgotten and the world for Meursault is (quite literally) good. This feeling of physical contentment continues throughout lunch. Meursault is "hungry … starving" (51); he takes great pleasure in the food, wine, coffee and cigarettes. Such is his contentment that he falls into the little robotic woman's error of seeking to control his life, "Masson, Raymond and I talked about spending August together at the beach, sharing expenses" (52).

The word which Meursault uses to describe his feelings as he swims with Marie is "happy," and it seems reasonable to apply the term to his feelings during the entire two-hour period between getting off of the bus and finishing lunch (50). Meursault's word choice is an important one to which he will return later in the narrative, but at this point it is vital to point out that, though his happiness is real, Meursault's understanding of its origin is mistaken. Whilst on the sand with Masson watching Marie swim, Meursault becomes "absorbed by the feeling that the sun was going me a lot of good" (50). Meursault's error becomes clear when we recall that this is the same sun which Meursault earlier perceived as an enemy, "the day, already bright with sun, hit me like a slap in the face" (47) and which he will later perceive as an antagonist "beating down on my bear head" (53). The inconsistency here is *not* the author's but the narrator's. The error is in the personification implied by each description (Ruskin's pathetic fallacy): in reality, the sun is not doing anything - the sun simply *is*. Happiness is possible under the sun, but it is also possible to be unhappy: the sun neither creates the happiness not does it prevent it. Meursault has made the error of raising the sun to the level of an external value. If any of these statements about the sun was right, then Meursault would have neither freedom of feeling, thought or (ultimately) action and thus no ability freely to choose happiness.

Mounting Social Pressures: Marriage

There is another ominous development during this apparently idyllic morning. The meeting with Sintès' friend Masson and his Parisian wife prompts Meursault to an important realization. It is the first experience Meursault has in the narrative of a married couple, and, as he sees Marie laughing with Masson's wife, the image of domesticity jolts him, "For the first time, maybe, I really thought I was going to get married" (50). Typically, Meursault (the man not given to self-reflection) offers no interpretation of his feeling; he simply records it. The reader, however, can see domesticity as one of the several ways in which social obligations have been closing in on Meursault from the moment he received news of the death of his mother. It is also significant that Masson's wife is from Paris. We have already seen in Chapter Five that Meursault dislikes Paris because it represents to him urban life and carries connotations of government authority - the very antithesis of the physicality and relative freedom of the *pied-noir* lifestyle which he (like Camus) so obviously enjoys. Meursault's feeling is reinforced by Masson's description after lunch of his domestic arrangements, "'My wife always takes a nap after lunch. Me, I don't like naps'" (52), and the fact that Marie stays with Madame Masson to clear away the dishes, thus acting out the domestic role she will play once she and Meursault are married. As McCarthy correctly points out, "Each time Meursault goes to the beach, it is to avoid remaining with the women" (McCarthy 48). Unfortunately, because he is Sintès' pal, going to the beach will bring him into conflict with the Arabs. He escapes one social entanglement only to be pulled into another.

Mounting Social Pressures: Pals

When Meursault leaves the cottage with Sintès and Masson to walk on the beach, his sensory experiences are immediately and dramatically negative. The sea which had earlier been "dazzling" (49) now reflects back a "glare" which is "unbearable" (52), and the sand which was "nice" when he earlier lay his face on it (51) now radiates a "rocky heat" which makes it "hard to breathe" (52); Meursault appears to be trapped between the heat from the sun and the heat from the sand. Once again, Meursault locates the source of his physical discomfort in an external force, the malignant sun, "I wasn't thinking about anything, because I was half asleep from the sun beating down on my bare head" (53). The personification makes Meursault appear to be a helpless victim, yet we know that sleep is an avoidance strategy which Meursault typically uses when confronted by unpleasant realities. Nevertheless, the reader is tempted to accept Meursault's explanation of his discomfort: it is, after all, the hottest part of the day and therefore considerably less comfortable than the pleasant sunshine which Meursault so enjoyed when he was on the beach earlier with Marie. The explanation is, however, illogical, since we recall that Meursault felt the sun as an antagonist in the early morning when objectively speaking it would have been much less hot.

The true explanation for Meursault's feelings lies in the growing social pressures which have been impacting him ever since the death of his mother. This is made clear when Masson notices the two Arabs, and Sintès confirms that they are the same Arabs seen earlier in the day in Algiers. Meursault is immediately forced into a situation where he feels obliged to act without being free to decide on how to act. Having no motivation of his own, Meursault can only agree to Sintès' order that, if another Arab appears, he must take him, "I said, 'Yes'" (53). It is immediately after having agreed to this that Meursault comments, "The blazing sand looked red to me now" (53). The careful juxtaposition by Camus locates the change of perception in Meursault's consciousness: the red symbolizes the anger and blood which his mind associates with the confrontation in which he has become embroiled.

The altercation which follows is described by Meursault in short, purely factual sentences as though he is simply an observer unrelated to the antagonists. This changes, however, when he gives Raymond a warning, "I shouted, 'Look out, he's got a knife!'" (54). By this action, Meursault gives up his separate identity. For the first time, the description offers some interpretation, "We didn't dare move," and the remainder of the description of the encounter is written in terms of two opposing groups: "they" and "us" (54). Meursault has been subsumed into the group of male pals; he has lost his separate identity and is no longer a stranger.

The Meaning of Freedom

The return to the bungalow involves Meursault being drawn back into the domestic group. He finds the women's emotional reaction to Sintès' relatively minor injuries as annoying as he found the mourners at Maman's vigil, and he takes refuge in silence and in trying to recapture positive sense impressions, "Madam Masson was crying and Marie was very pale. I didn't like having to explain to them, so I just shut up, smoked a cigarette, and looked at the sea" (54). This is the same avoidance strategy which Meursault has used throughout the novel when confronted with social situations which seem to require from him an emotional, or at least, an engaged, response.

Meursault will go back to the beach twice more; two self-destructive decisions which he appears not to recognize as self-destructive. When Sintès returns from visiting the doctor, he announces his intention to go down to the beach, clearly determined to re-new his confrontation with the Arabs. He gets angry when Masson and Meursault suggest that they accompany him, but Meursault decides to follow him anyway. Showalter correctly identifies this as "Meursault's first rejection of authority, almost his first willful act in the novel" (39). This action is unexplained, but two factors in Meursault's motivation are his desire to escape the domestic atmosphere in the bungalow and his sense of obligation as Raymond's pal.

Immediately he sets foot on the beach, Meursault is overwhelmed by negative sense impressions, "By now the sun was overpowering. It shattered into little pieces on the sand and water" (55). This image of disintegration is the very opposite of the harmony which Meursault has at times thought to exist between the human and natural worlds. The "low gurgling" of the water gushing from the spring offers no relief from the heat, and the three notes which the Arab plays on his reed (sounds not in themselves unpleasant) are repeated threateningly "over and over again" (55). Meursault describes "the sound of the water and the flute" paradoxically as being "deep within the silence and the heat" which conveys the oppressive nature of the sun (56).

Moral Imperatives

When Sintès finds the two Arabs, he is clearly intent on revenge. Despite the fact that the Arabs appear "perfectly calm and almost content," he reaches into his pocket for his revolver with the clear intention of shooting one or both of them. Interestingly, given what will happen later on the beach, Meursault uses a number of calmly stated moral arguments to dissuade Raymond from firing his gun. Meursault's arguments derive from the law and from Meursault's innate sense of fairness: it would be "'pretty lousy'" to shoot a man who has not even made any kind of verbal threat; you "'can't'" shoot a man unless he has drawn a knife; you should not use a gun on an unarmed adversary, but should instead "'take him on man to man'" (56). At this point in the narrative, Meursault clearly feels that moral imperatives exist and not that one action is as valid as another action; it is the only time in the novel that he will speak in this way. He is actually using the language of authority, the language of the director, the priest, the boss, the police and the judicial system. This indicates the extent to which his integration into various social groups (engaged people, pals, us) has stopped him from being an outside, a stranger.

Meursault's First Epiphany

Meursault's reasoning has the desired effect, and Raymond hands him the revolver. However, almost immediately Meursault has an epiphany which completely invalidates the moral reasoning he has just used so effectively. Once again, it is prompted by the sense that life happens in an isolated confrontation between man and a hostile environment, "We stared at each other without blinking, and everything came to a stop there between the sea, the sand, and the sun, and the double silence of the flute and the water. It was then that I realized that you could either shoot or not shoot" (56). The unaware man has an epiphany, or at least a partial epiphany: he comes to understand that humans are entirely free agents because there *are* no moral imperatives.

Meursault consciously articulates for the first time the insignificance of human existence and therefore of any action. He locates his revelation precisely in the confrontation between man and "the sea, the sand, and the sun, and the double silence of the flute and the water" (56). This is an example of what McCarthy calls Camus' "discourse on the sun composed in lyrical language" (45) which he finds "unsatisfactory because it

101

cannot be translated into the language of the rest of the book" (46). It is a fair point, but perhaps McCarthy overestimates the difficulty of such passages. Here, Meursault appears to come face-to-face with his own mortality: the sea, sun and sand will endure and a man will not. For this reason, the sea, sun and sand are perceived as hostile, and against their hostility the music of the flute (human endeavor) and the cooling of the water (sensual pleasure) are helpless.

Meursault is fully aware that he has come to an understanding of the human condition which makes his earlier moral arguments irrelevant: man has complete freedom of action, and "'can't'" has been superseded in Meursault's language by "'could.'" The loss of a life will have no significance; it *can* have no effect on life as a whole because the world is totally hostile to everything. Given that every man dies, how can it possibly matter *when* a single man dies? This perception implicitly denies the existence of God, and thus denies transcendent moral values. Meursault is no longer the unaware man who told his boss that "one life was as good as another" but could not explain why he felt this to be true (41). However, he has made only the first step on the path of understanding the absurd life. At this point, Meursault has neither the opportunity nor the need to act upon his new-found understanding (that will come later in the afternoon) because the two Arabs back away from the confrontation.

Asserting One's Freedom

When they return to the bungalow, Meursault feels himself to be faced by two impossible alternatives: to climb the steps and re-enter the emotionally charged domestic situation, specifically to "face the women again," or to stay in the intense heat "standing still in the blinding stream falling from the sky" (57). In this situation, Meursault applies his new understanding of man's freedom: he can either stay or he can go. However, Meursault is convinced that man's freedom exists in a hostile world which makes all human choices meaningless, "To stay or to go, it amounted to the same thing" (57). Thus, turning his

102

back on his relationships with Marie and with Sintès, he decides to return to the beach.

Bloom comments, "This philosophy, which others in the book have found exasperating when Meursault gives voice to it, does not seem to hold true by the end of the chapter. How different Meursault's life might have been had be not walked down the beach by himself" (Bloom ed. 36). At this point in the development of his awareness, Meursault is unconsciously taking the position of Dostoyevsky that if God does not exist then everything is possible. Unfortunately, Meursault's reasoning is faulty. He accurately perceives that man is free and that laws, social relationships and internalized moral concepts are meaningless because death makes them so, but he makes the mistake of assuming that this necessarily makes choice a value-free (and consequence-free) activity.

It is simply not true that to stay at the house or to leave it amount to the same thing because actions have consequences; equally, though a man may at any moment decide to shoot or not to shoot, these two actions most certainly do not amount to the same thing. So why does Meursault make the mistake of assuming that they do? The reason is that he has misunderstood the context in which actions (and, even more importantly, decisions about actions) are taken. For Meursault, human society has become intolerable because it appears to be making intolerable demands upon him: he is expected to mourn when he feels no sadness; to seem ambitious when he is perfectly content with a clerk's job; to feel love when he just wants to enjoy sexual contact; to be loyal to a man who beats up women; to feel morally offended when a man mistreats his dog.

At the same time, the physical world appears to him as an antagonist, "All that heat was pressing down on me and making it hard for me to go on. And every time I felt a blast of its hot breath strike my face, I gritted my teeth, clenched my fists in my trouser pockets, and strained ever nerve to overcome the sun and the thick drunkenness it was spilling over me" (57). The description here is an example of anthropomorphic supernaturalism: the personification of the sun as an adversary is reinforced by the use of strong active verbs to describe an encounter where Meursault feels himself to be the helpless victim. Having quite rightly rejected the transcendent values which conventionally underpin Western society, Meursault has made the error of assuming that we therefore live a valueless life in a hostile world. Accepting this premise, Meursault is caught in the greatest Catch 22 of them all: man is entirely free, but, since all choices are of equal value, his freedom is completely meaningless.

Summary:

A satisfactory reading of Chapter 6 must explain the significance of the sun in a consistent way.

Meursault alternates between feeling that the sun is an antagonist and feeling that it is benevolent. Both perceptions are fundamental errors.

Meursault feels happy when he is free to enjoy the sensual pleasures of the day but unhappy when placed under pressure by other characters to conform to their expectations.

Meursault projects his feelings onto his environment – specifically he anthropomorphizes the sun.

Meursault comes to understand that man is entirely free to choose his actions.

Given man's mortality, Meursault is convinced that one choice is the same as another.

PART ONE Chapter 6 (continued): Meursault Fires Five Shots

> There is but one truly serious philosophical problem and that is suicide. Judging whether life is or is not worth living amounts to answering the fundamental question of philosophy. (Camus *Myth* 3)

1. Why does Meursault shoot the Arab man the first time?

2. Why does he then fire four times into the man's body?

3. Is his reaction to what he has done typical or untypical of him?

Autobiographical Background

Camus based the shooting which is the climax of Part One on an actual incident involving his friend Raoul Bensoussan which occurred on the beach at Bouisseville outside Oran. Camus was not himself present, but he heard the story many times. It appears that Raoul Bensoussan was involved in a verbal altercation with two Arabs who he met by chance on the beach. When he returned to his friends, Raoul told the story to his brother, and the two of them went back to the scene of the argument. A fight ensued in which Raoul was injured by one of the Arabs who had a knife. Olivier Todd concludes the story, "That afternoon, during lunch by the seaside, Raoul resolved to have his revenge, and armed with a small-caliber automatic pistol, he went looking for the two Arabs ..." (Todd 99). No final confrontation appears to have resulted.

Camus made two significant changes in adapting this incident for his novel. In the first place, whilst Raoul undoubtedly took the handgun to the beach with the intention of using it, it is by no means clear in the novel what Meursault's intentions in returning to the beach are or even how aware he is that he still has Sintès' gun. Secondly, in the real-life incident, the two Arabs were arrested by the police and eventually charged with the relatively minor offence of disturbing the peace since the Bensoussan brothers did not press charges against them (Todd 100).

The Problem of Interpretation

The shooting of the Arab by Meursault is one of the most controversial incidents in twentieth century literature, and any interpretation of *The Stranger* must explain its significance. Camus has been bitterly criticized for including this incident on the grounds that the Arab is a human being like Meursault with his own hopes and dreams, yet he seems to be treated by the author as a mere cipher or plot device. Even more damning has been the charge that the author appears to ignore the racist nature of this action: the murder of an Arab by a *pied noir* has a colonialist dimension which, in his life, Camus was well aware of, but which the novel seems unwilling to face even as Camus exploits it to add to those social pressures which make Meursault feel that he is completely trapped. However, these criticisms rest upon the assumption that the novel presents the murder as in some way acceptable, and this is *not* the case.

Many readers empathize with Meursault from the very start of the novel. They share his implicit criticism of society and his desire to have no part of society's comic pantomime. The reader should remember, however, that the shooting is described in the first person, and Meursault is the novel's protagonist/narrator and not the author. A careful reading of the text shows that Camus provides a context which indicates the error that Meursault is making. Put briefly, Meursault mistakes the liberating effect of the absurd for authorization: it *is* true that at any moment a man *may* choose to shoot or not to shoot, but that truth does *not* mean that the decision to shoot lacks an ethical dimension.

Some critics take the view that it is impossible to explain Meursault's action in shooting the Arab; that Camus' whole point is that Meursault has no reason; and that, in trying to discover one, the reader is deliberately drawn by the author into replicating the futility of the court's attempts to find order and meaning in a life which is random. Certainly analyses which seek to explain Meursault's action in terms of conventional character analysis invariably appear to be based upon a consciousness created for Meursault by the critic rather than on the evidence (or lack of evidence) of Meursault's narrative itself. The following extract will stand as an example:

> Meursault's apathy toward life and the repressed rage that erupts when he shoots the Arab five times may result from the failure to achieve his goals despite his intelligence and education … And it may be that rage at his boring job and the failure, because of factors beyond his control, to complete his education and fulfill his ambitions precipitate Meursault's act of violence. Disgust with himself for getting involved with a disreputable person such as Raymond may have forced his hand, causing him to pull the trigger – a last desperate means of wrenching himself free of a degrading entanglement. (Scherr 151).

There is much in what Scherr writes which is obviously true, particularly the insight that Meursault acts out of "repressed rage that erupts." However, the error which Scherr makes by locating the source of this rage in the thwarted ambition of an intelligent man is the same kind of error that the court will make when it puts Meursault on trial for his crime: both attempt to rationalize and understand the shooting in terms of cause and effect because to accept the shooting as an entirely random act is to accept that our attempts to make life meaningful are a failure. The result is what S.T.Coleridge in another context termed "the motive-hunting of motiveless Malignity." The truth is, however, that what Meursault does is neither explicable in terms of criminal psychology nor is it presented by Camus as simply random: the truth is both more complex and more interesting.

The Significance of the Shooting of the Arab

The shooting of the Arab has its origin in the change to Meursault's life which begins with the telegram announcing the death of his mother. Meursault's life in the years between placing this mother in Marengo and her death are presented as (given his particular needs and limitations) virtually idyllic: he has a satisfying job, a set routine, a flirtation with Marie, and, above all, no emotional demands. The telegram changes all of that: it drags Meursault out of his comfort zone by placing emotional demands upon him to which he is ill-equipped to respond. Meursault is placed in social situations (viewing the body, the vigil, and the burial) where others define his reactions and create a social identity for him that he feels compelled to accept. This is compounded by the renewal and intensification of his relationship with Marie who begins to demand commitment by talking about love and marriage, the pressure from his boss to move to Paris, being manipulated into a conspiracy by the pimp Sintès, and the increasing familiarity of Salamano.

Everything comes to a head during this day at the beach where Meursault beings to feel the combined pressures of the criminal activity and of the domestic situation in which he has allowed himself to become entangled as intolerable constraints on his freedom and attacks on his identity. Having turned his back on both by deciding not to climb the stairs and re-enter the house, Meursault, as so often, seeks refuge in the prospect of sensual gratification. The following sentence references touch, hearing and vision, "I was thinking of the <u>cool</u> spring behind the rock. I wanted to <u>hear</u> the murmur of its water again, to escape the sun and the strain and the women's tears, and to find <u>shade</u> and rest again at last" (emphasis added 57). This quotation makes it clear that Meursault's decision to return to the beach is yet another avoidance strategy, an attempt to evade the "strain" of the social world and luxuriate in sensual gratification. However, in the midday heat, he has come to feel that the physical world is antagonistic and oppressive because he has unconsciously projected his unhappiness *onto* the physical world. He literally objectifies his psychological trauma in the sun.

A man who instinctively (and now intellectually) believes in free will, Meursault has come to feel that his freedom has been eroded. Although he is not consciously aware of his motivation, he shoots the Arab to prove the proposition that "you could either shoot or not shoot" *because* he is beginning to doubt it, or rather to doubt that man's freedom can change anything (56). The shooting is reactive not proactive. The closest Meursault himself ever comes to explaining why he fires the shots will be his statement to the court, "realizing how ridiculous I sounded, I blurted out that it was because of the sun" which highlights the reactive nature of his motivation (103). Thus, Meursault is certainly motivated by "repressed rage," but it is rage against an "absurd godless world" (*Myth* 92) not against thwarted ambition, and his rage takes the form of *suicide*.

What Meursault is doing is deliberately taking a course of action which will end at once the illusions of meaning which every other character in the novel has constructed in order to avoid confrontation with the absurd. The point is made most clearly in Camus' *Myth of Sisyphus*, "Dying voluntarily implies that you have recognized, even instinctively, the ridiculous character of that habit, the absence of any profound reason for living, the insane character of that daily agitation, and the uselessness of suffering" (6). This precisely describes Meursault's mental state at the time of the shooting.

Michael Delahoyde sums up Meursault's actions as originating in "his detatched [*sic*], passive, and psychotic nature … His disconnection is true madness, for he knows what he is doing, senses the repercussions, yet in a trance-like state, continues … although the sun may have served as an irritant and a factor in his actions, the actual act of killing comes from his innate disconnection with reality." Again, there is much here with which to agree: the essentially passive nature of Meursault's action; the fact that the action is taken with full knowledge of its social and legal consequences; the fact that the sun is merely an "irritant." However, any analysis which suggests that Meursault is insane at the moment of the shooting because he is disconnected from "reality" must be rejected as contrary to Camus' intention. The fact is that Meursault is more nearly aware of the "reality" of human existence at this point than is any other character in the novel - more nearly aware and, consequently, more terrified.

How an Arab Comes to be Shot

Having returned to the beach house following the second confrontation with the Arabs, Meursault knows that he is entirely free to choose between two courses of action: he can climb the stairs and face again the emotional reaction of the women, or he can stay on the beach in the extreme heat of the midday sun. Not surprisingly, Meursault decides that in such circumstances the concept of a free choice becomes meaningless, "the heat was so intense that it was just as bad standing still in the blinding stream falling from the sky. To stay or to go, it amounted to the same thing" (57). Something essential has changed about Meursault here. He is no longer merely a stranger alienated from society; he is now alienated from human existence itself, feeling that every aspect of life is vicious. There is simply no choice available to Meursault which holds out the prospect of happiness. Showalter sums it up this way, "Meursault has followed the consequences of his perception of meaninglessness all the way to nihilism" (103).

The sun appears to Meursault as an enemy, and he uses the language of assault to describe it. He writes that "[the] heat was pressing down on me ... I felt a blast of its hot breath strike my face ... every blade of light"; even the sea, which has previously offered a delightfully cool escape from the heat of the sun, now appears to be equally its victim, "[t]he sea gasped for air" (57). Typically, Meursault does what he always does in moments of stress, he seeks to take refuge in pleasant sensation as when he drank coffee with milk and smoked at Maman's vigil to avoid the grief of the mourners, or when he smoked and looked at the sea earlier in this chapter to avoid the women's hysterical reaction to Sintès' injury. Now, he seeks escape by "thinking of the cool spring behind the rock. I wanted to hear the murmur of its water again, to escape the sun and the strain and the women's tears, and to find shade and rest again at last" (57). The gentle diction used to describe the pool references touch, hearing and sight ("cool ... murmur ... shade") contrasts with the violent diction used to describe the sun. Julian Stamm explains that at this moment Meursault "is seeking a haven or retreat from the memories of the mother and the strain and effort of masculine responsibility that would be entailed in the threatening, deepening relationship with Marie" (quoted in Gay-Crosier 145). The fact that Meursault wishes to find "rest again" indicates that he wishes to return to that idyllic period before he became involved with Sintès and Marie, indeed back to the time before the telegram which announced Maman's death because his life has been nothing but "strain" since that point, and now it has become unbearable.

For Meursault, however, there is no going back: he sees himself as literally trapped in time, "It was the same sun, the same light still shining on the same sand as before. For two hours the day had stood still; for two hours it had been anchored in a sea of molten lead" (58). He is trapped because the Arab is in the same position as he was two hours ago, suggesting that although Meursault feels that "the whole thing was over" it is not: he has got himself involved in a conflict which he is powerless to end (58). He is trapped because he cannot return to Marie since now he realizes that he is "going to get married" and has seen how intolerable that will be (50). He is trapped because the physical world, which has always provided positive sensual experiences to balance the negative, appears to have turned against him, not least because its timelessness reminds him of his own mortality.

In this situation, Meursault thinks once again that he is free to walk away, "It occurred to me that all I had to do was turn around and that would be the end of it" (50). Note that this perception is not hindsight; the narrator clearly identifies it as something which he understood at the time. However, it is patently not true: it is not true of the social entanglements into which Meursault has become enmeshed, and it is not true of his situation as a mortal man in relation to the eternal "sun ... light ... sand." Walking away will change nothing about the human condition.

The only possible relief which Meursault perceives is the spring, towards which he takes a few steps, but the spring is where the Arab is so that a confrontation is inevitable. In the extreme heat, Meursault's head begins to throb as the blood rushes through his body as it did at Maman's funeral ("I could feel the blood pounding in my temples" [17]) and again on leaving the apartment of Sintès after having written the letter for him ("All I could hear was the blood pounding in my ears" [33]). As then, the cause of the pounding in Meursault's head, which makes it impossible for him to think clearly, is the "strain" of social pressures which he projects onto the sun. Now Meursault objectifies everything in the sun, "I could feel my forehead swelling under the sun ... my forehead especially was hurting me, all the veins in it throbbing under the skin" (57-9). The result is that a man who has just understood man's freedom ("you could either shoot or not shoot" [56]) becomes convinced that the freedom he has is meaningless, "It was this burning, which I couldn't stand anymore, that made me move forward. I knew it was stupid, that I wouldn't get the sun off me by stepping forward. But, I took a step, one step, forward" (emphasis added 59). In this comment, Meursault the narrator explains to the reader his feelings at the time he took the decisive move forward using hindsight to state things more clearly than Meursault the protagonist would have been able to do at the time. Looking back, Meursault describes his action as illogical, his attempt to escape as self-destructive since it results in inevitable conflict with the Arab. Even at the time he senses this intuitively.

In Meursault's perception, the Arab (the social world) and the sun (the natural world) become one as the sun is reflected off of the Arab's knife. Once again, the language of assault is used, "light shot off the steel … like a long flashing blade cutting at my forehead … the cymbals of sunlight crashing on my forehead … the dazzling spear flying up from the knife … The scorching blade slashed at my eyelashes and stabbed at my stinging eyes" (59). That is when the first shot fires, "[t]he trigger gave" (59). It is almost an unconscious action, certainly a reaction to intolerable pressure, and not in any sense a response to actual danger posed by the Arab. Meursault describes it as something which happened rather than as something which he did.

Meursault the narrator makes it clear that immediately after the shot Meursault the protagonist understands what he has done and why he has done it, "I knew that I had shattered the harmony of the day, the exceptional silence of a beach where I'd been happy" (59). Standing over the body of the dead Arab, Meursault understands that his action is an implicit rejection of the happiness which he has found in life. Weighed against the "strain" of a social world into which he knows he does not fit, and against a physical world which appears to him to be his enemy, the brief happinesses of life appear to be accidental and insignificant, which is why he fires again, "Then I fired four more times at the motionless body where the bullets lodged without leaving a trace. And it was like knocking four quick times on the door of unhappiness" (59). The simile "it was like knocking four quick times on the door of unhappiness" (59) is Camus' way of linking the murder to Meursault's relationship with Sintès for at the start of this chapter Meursault records that on their way down from his apartment, he and Marie "knocked on Raymond's door" (47). Notice the shift to active verbs "fired …knocking". Once again, the lucid interpretation belongs to Meursault the narrator, but he is accurately explaining what he felt at the time. By shooting the Arab, Meursault makes the statement that he does not value happiness in his life; in firing the final four shots, he deliberately, consciously cuts himself off from the happiness he has had in his life by putting himself entirely in the hands of the state. Firing the last four shots is not a freely chosen action but a negative and self-destructive act of rebellion, and it is not presented as acceptable: just because you *could* shoot does not mean that you *should* choose to shoot.

How the Shooting Changes Everything for Meursault

Brée concludes that, "with the shooting, something has gone irrevocably wrong, Meursault knows immediately, though neither what nor why" (*Albert Camus* 18). In the rest of the novel, whilst the action concerns society's determination to condemn Meursault, the philosophy is directed to answering these two questions. However complex Meursault's motivation in shooting the Arab may be, its consequences are clear to Meursault even at the moment he fires the final four shots: the shooting fundamentally changes his relationship to and hence his understanding of mortality. From the moment that Meursault fires the first shot, his own death becomes an imminent reality. The narrator clearly draws the reader's attention to his use of hindsight to highlight this change when he writes, "The trigger gave; ... and there in that noise, sharp and deafening at the same time, is where it all started" (emphasis added 59). Here Camus uses the narrator to indicate that Part One is merely a preamble, a necessary introduction to the true psychological drama (one might say philosophical drama) which is the main interest of the novel. Robert Zaretsky precisely defines the difference between the manner of Meursault's existence before and after the shooting:

> 'It' for Meursault is what was, is, and will be for most of us: life measured by an artificial conception of time. From a kind of time-less existence – he is uncertain about the date of his mother's death, as he is about her age when she died – an inexorable and steady justice overtakes Meursault's life. Until the moment he pulls the trigger, Meursault is as indifferent to the future as he is to the past. He does not puzzle over his life – events, indeed, are not pieces to a puzzle, for there is no puzzle to piece together. Instead, 'life' is a word for the waves of

physical sensations that wash over him as constantly as the sunlight and the sea. (54)

By the end of Pert One, Meursault has decided that life is not worth living.

Part Two of the novel will chronicle Meursault's difficult evolution towards consciousness. In Part One, Meursault is intuitively aware of the absurdity of human existence. This determines the almost random way in which he lives a life in which the only things he finds to be real and true are his physical experiences, and it results in the indefensible murder of another human being. In Part Two, Meursault's forced introspection about his life and its meaning while contemplating his impending death by formal execution leads him to acknowledge his mortality and thus to accept responsibility for living his own life.

Summary:

Meursault goes back to the spring to find a refuge from the "strains" of the social and the physical worlds.

Meursault perceives the sun as an antagonist because he unconsciously sees it as an embodiment of the pressures which are making his life intolerable.

Having escaped the pressures of society, he encounters on the beach the most fundamental of these pressures in his growing awareness of his own mortality in contrast to the immortality of the physical world.

Meursault shoots the Arab as an act of defiance, of revolt.

The shooting is Meursault's conscious rejection of happiness; it is a form of suicide.

PART TWO Chapter 1: Interrogation

On the surface, *L'Etranger* gives the appearance of being an extremely simple though carefully planned and written book. In reality, it is a dense and rich creation, full of undiscovered meanings and formal qualities. It would take a book at least the length of the novel to make a complete analysis of meaning and form and the correspondences of meaning and form, in *L'Etranger*. (Carl A. Viggiani, 1956)

Consider the following:

1. Give some examples of the way in which Meursault focuses on the practical details of his life in prison rather than on its emotional elements. How does this tendency lead him to make a number of inappropriate responses to his situation?

2. How does Meursault answer the charge that he "had 'shown insensitivity' the day of Maman's funeral" (64)?

3. Meursault frequently claims that he is "like everyone else" (66), "the same as anyone" (67). How do the people to whom he is telling this react? How do you react? Is he right?

4. What reasons does Meursault give for failing to respond to being questioned about the pause between his first and second shot that he fired at the Arab?

5. On being asked by the magistrate if he is sorry for murdering the Arab man, Meursault replies "that more than sorry I felt kind of annoyed. I got the impression he didn't understand" (70). Explain Meursault's meaning here.

6. Explain how Meursault's atheism and his indifference to his mother's death challenge the magistrate's belief in a rational world controlled by God - the belief that gives his life meaning. How does the magistrate adapt to this perceived challenge so that he is soon able to treat Meursault in a cordial way

The Relationship between Parts One and Two of the Novel

Carl A. Viggiani calls *The Stranger* a "carefully planned and written book." This statement is supported both by biographical evidence and from a study of the structure of the novel itself. However, the novel which Camus finally published is far from being a perfect work of art. As we have seen, many critics find Meursault's motives for firing the five shots at the Arab to be obscure. René Girard frankly concludes that "'our efforts to make sense of Meursault's criminal action get nowhere'" (quoted in McCarthy 50). In response to these criticisms, the last two chapters offered an interpretation of Meursault's action which makes sense both in terms of his psychological development and of the symbolism of the sun and heat which Camus uses throughout the novel. We must turn now, however, to the transition from Part One to Part Two which confronts the reader with a structural problem which does indeed weaken the novel.

The essential problem of *The Stranger* is generally seen to be the discontinuity between Parts One and Two. Camus is a "philosophical writer ... in the sense that he has (a) conceived his own distinctive and original world view and (b) sought to convey that view mainly through images, fictional characters and events, and dramatic presentation" (Simpson). As a result, *The Stranger* is a novel of ideas, and as such it suffers from a problem inherent with the genre: the ideas tend to take precedence over all other aspects of the novel, particularly plot and characterization. Camus' aim in Part Two is to expose to withering criticism the authority of society; it is the legal system that prosecutes and convicts Meursault which is actually on trial in Part Two. Naturally, given Camus' philosophical position, society's imposition of its values of law and justice must be shown to be fraudulent, whilst Meursault's perception that these values have no validity must be vindicated. As a result, Part Two is in some respects a very different kind of novel: there is, for example, a great deal of satirical comedy which is entirely absent in Part One. Brée highlights "Meursault's semiburlesque interviews with the prosecutor, magistrate, and lawyer" (*Albert Camus* 18) and McCarthy writes that, "The second half of *The Stranger* may be read as a comic novel" which may be understood as exaggeration to make a point because there is much besides comedy in Part Two (65).

At the end of the novel, Meursault will reach a world view which the novel will essentially endorse, and therefore the reader must be able to empathize with the Camus' protagonist, and here is Camus' problem because Meursault has murdered another human being in cold blood. Not only that, but at no time does he show any remorse for having done so, which would seem to make it impossible for the reader to sympathize with him rather than with the legal system which condemns a guilty man to death. That, in a nutshell, is the structural challenge which Camus faces in Part Two.

The Disappearing Arab

Camus' solution to the problem of making the reader see things at the end of the novel from Meursault's point of view is, as Meursault's trial progresses, to increasingly shift the focus of the narrative away from the murder of the Arab and towards the way Meursault lived his life prior to the shooting (and particularly to his failure to grieve for his mother's death). The result is that, as McCarthy points out, "the Arab plays no role at all, his death becoming – like his life and his sister's life – a non-event" (54). The Arab victim virtually disappears from Part Two; in fact, not one Arab character appears in Part Two following Marie's one visit to Meursault in Chapter 3. Camus controls the process so well that many readers hardly notice it happening, but if McCarthy is correct in arguing that "the murder of the Arab is a pretext that allows Meursault to be condemned while retaining the reader's sympathy," then in using this artistic legerdemain Camus is guilty of more than poor construction. He has actually exploited the inherent racism of his readers in the cause of vindicating Meursault by assuming that they will be complicit in making the Arab disappear (remember that the novel was published in 1945), and the artistic integrity of the novel is severely damaged.

The attacks on Camus' depiction of the Arab victim take many forms. Lottman comments that an (unnamed) historian interpreted *The Stranger* "as the symbol of the Algerian Frenchman isolated in his Moslem milieu" and that an (again unnamed) "hostile Algerian would decide that in killing the Arab, Camus (or his hero) subconsciously acted out the dream of the *pied noir* who loved Algeria but without [Moslem] Algerians" (244). Several critics (most notably Conor Cruise O'Brien) have attacked the way in which Meursault's trial is presented by pointing out that at the time the novel is set no *pied noir* would have been convicted and sentenced to death for the killing of an armed Arab. (If the analogy is helpful, it is about as realistic as it would have been if Harper Lee had allowed Atticus Finch to win an acquittal for Tom Robinson in *To Kill a Mockingbird*!) Camus is forced to be unhistorical because his ideas demand that Meursault must be convicted, for without a conviction there would be no basis for criticism of the judicial system. In order to get his protagonist into the position of victim, he must ignore the political realities of colonial Algeria.

All such criticisms make the assumption that Camus is (or that he should be) writing realism in *The Stranger*, a conclusion which is perfectly understandable because so much in the novel appears to be grounded in the day-to-day lives of the characters. However, this study has argued that the setting of *The Stranger* is only *nominally* French Colonial Algeria. At times, it seems that the setting is no more intended to be a real country at a particular time than are the settings for Kafka's *The Trial* and *The Castle*, yet in the majority of the novel the characters' lives are rendered realistically, and this is particularly true of the account of the French judicial process which Camus understood well from his time as a newspaper reporter covering trials in Algeria. Nevertheless, Camus is not aiming for absolute realism.

It is true that Camus exploits racial tensions in Algeria in his presentation of the conflict between Raymond Sintès and the Arab brother of the woman he beats up, but racial differences are hardly essential to the plot. Even Meursault's shooting of the Arab, although it can certainly be interpreted in colonialism terms (see McCarthy 50-1), appears from Meursault's account of it to have nothing to do with fact that his victim is an Arab. The fact is that Camus uses his intimate knowledge of Algeria and its people selectively: when it suits his purpose, he reflects reality in meticulous detail, but when reality conflicts with the ideas for which the novel is but a vehicle, then reality is simply ignored. Camus' justification would be that the central concern of the novel is universal and transcends the socio-political situation in a particular country at a particular time.

How Camus Actually Uses the Setting of the Novel

The Stranger does move inconsistently from one world to another: Part One must inevitably be read, at least partly, as a novel of colonial occupation, but Part Two deals with universal issues of being. In Part Two, Meursault is brought fact-to-face with French institutions in the form of the police and the legal system. Since it is Camus' intention to present these social and political institutions as arbitrary and meaningless, it actually strengthens his case that these very institutions are imposed upon a Muslim majority by an anti-democratic ruling minority. It can be argued that it is the legal process, not Camus, which virtually excludes the Arabs not one of whom is called to testify. In this sense, the murdered Arab is as much a victim of the inauthentic French legal system as is Meursault. Various critics have pointed out that Meursault being a stranger alienated from society is in much the same position as the Arabs – both are silent watchers of a system from which they feel excluded. This parallel is hinted at in this chapter, but it is soon dropped.

Those who feel that Camus should have written an anti-colonialist novel will find his selective use of the real Algeria to be inexcusable. The French legal system, however, is merely used by Camus as an exemplar to symbolize the absurdity that lies in humanity's futile attempt to find rational order where none exists: individual lives, the life of society, and human existence in general have no rational meaning or order. Because people find this truth too frightening, they attempt to identify or to create rational structure and meaning in their lives. This absurdity is seen at its clearest in society's attempt to give meaning to Meursault's crime by creating a justice system which will explain his motivations, find them to be anti-social and immoral, and punish his deviance with capital punishment. Camus is making a universal point which applies to the judicial systems of all nations, and therefore to identify his criticisms too closely with French Colonial justice would actually weaken the essential point that he is making.

Mocking the Legal System:

Throughout Part One, Meursault has been the innocent, naive observer of a social structure which he has not understood, but following his arrest he is plunged into a judicial system of which he has no previous experience, so that while Meursault has always been prone to misjudge the actions of others this tendency is now significantly increased. Bloom remarks that he "shows a lack of awareness that seems to contradict his portrait as an intelligent and perceptive individual" (Bloom ed. 37). Psychological consistency has been sacrificed to the need to advance the author's ideas.

This inconsistency in Camus' presentation of Meursault's character is another consequence of the change in focus in Part Two. For Meursault to be an effective commentator on the absurdities of the system, Camus needs his narrator to be completely naïve. Thus, Meursault's account of the days following his arrest is made unintentionally comic: his reaction to the things he learns about the system is almost childlike. For example, he records his not entirely accurate perception that his initial round of questioning by the examining magistrate "was just so they could find out who I was" (63). Meursault does not realize the parallel between being asked Maman's age by the man from the undertaker's and by his boss and his being asked here "name and address, my occupation, the date and place of my birth" (63). These are questions which fix his identity as defined by the state. Because such details seem to him to be trivial, Meursault finds it impossible to take this stage in the questioning seriously. He does not realize that the state is asserting its power over him.

Meursault says that he thinks that his case is "pretty simple," and he appears impressed with the efficiency of the legal system when he is told that the state will provide him with a lawyer, "I thought it was very convenient that the court should take care of those details" (63). Meursault's trusting assumption that he is now in the hands of a benevolent system, is the beginning of Camus' strategy for winning the reader's sympathy for his protagonist.

Meursault's Detachment

An important aspect of Meursault's child-like naiveté is his failure to comprehend the true significance of the judicial process which has been started; it seems to him like a scene from a crime novel or "like a game," and he asserts that he does not at first take the examining magistrate seriously, finding him to be "very reasonable and, overall, very pleasant" (64). At the end of their meeting, Meursault only prevents himself from shaking the man's hand by recalling that he has killed a man.

The entire interrogation process takes about a year, and significantly at the end of it Meursault is no closer to seeing that he is caught in a process which will lead inevitably to his execution. Thus, when the magistrate tells him that he has never known a criminal who has not wept at the sight of the suffering Christ on the crucifix, Meursault comments, "I was about to say that that was precisely because they were criminals. But then I realized that I was one too. It was an idea I couldn't get used to" (70). Meursault's reaction can be judged on two levels. Firstly, it is proof of his naïve detachment. Secondly, it is inherently a revolt against the authority of the French judicial system. At the moment, Meursault's limited self-awareness will not allow him to articulate that revolt. Thus, when the magistrate asks if he is sorry for what he has done, Meursault replies "that I was more than sorry I felt kind of annoyed. I got the impression that he didn't understand" (70). What the magistrate does not understand is that Meursault feels no moral guilt over the shooting. Why should he, since one could either shoot or not shoot? He judges his action only on the basis of the inconvenient consequences which it has had for himself. The most that he appears to have realized is that actions do have consequences.

The entire development of Part Two involves Meursault coming to understand that his life now has not an indeterminate end-point in some distant future but a definite termination at a point in time which is rapidly approaching. The first part of that development will be his slowly growing awareness that (with all its comic absurdity) his trial is actually a matter of life and death – his life and death. Part One concentrates on the plot development whereby Meursault arrives at the beach where he shoots the Arab; Part Two examines the psychological development by which Meursault comes to an understanding of what it means to live knowing that death makes life meaningless.

Meursault and Humanism

When Meursault is informed by his lawyer that "there had been some investigations into my private life," it becomes clear to the reader that Camus is using the device of the crime novel genre in order to examine not a single crime but Meursault's entire way of living (64). The defense lawyer, himself a representative of the society which is placing Meursault on trial (he is formally dressed, despite the heat, as the director of the home had been), is both frustrated and angry at his client's honesty. The reader notes in Meursault a new-found assertiveness. He tells his lawyer that he "has pretty much lost the habit of analyzing" himself; that he "probably did love Maman, but that [it] didn't mean anything"; that his nature is such that his "physical needs often get in the way of" his feelings; and finally that it would not be true to say that at Maman's funeral he "held back my natural feelings" (65). This is the language of dissent, and, as Showalter points out, it is "by no means consistent" with his conduct at the funeral where "Meursault makes a considerable effort to conduct himself in an appropriate fashion ... his being there at all can be explained only by a sense of obligation to show filial respect' (64). At no time during this conversation does Meursault feel guilty about what he says or feel that he has said anything inappropriate, both of which he did repeatedly in Part One. This uncompromising honesty reminds the reader of his reply to Marie when she asks if he loves her, but whilst Marie laughs off Meursault's answer, his lawyer takes him seriously and Meursault comments that, "He gave me a strange look, as if he found me slightly disgusting" (65).

Meursault poses a threat to the entire civil system which his lawyer serves because, simply by existing, Meursault exposes the fact that that world is based upon self-deception. Meursault instinctively recognizes this and is able to articulate his understanding when he comments, "Mostly, I could tell, I made him feel uncomfortable. He didn't understand me, and he was sort of holding it against me. I felt the urge to reassure him that I was like everybody else, just like everybody else" (66). The comic irony of this statement is that it is precisely the fear that Meursault *is* actually normal which unsettles his lawyer. Society must prove that Meursault is a "monster" or accept that all of its members are monsters, and it is this that society cannot do (96).

The account of the interview with the lawyer is carefully presented by Camus so as to win the reader's sympathy for Meursault. In contrast to the lawyer's willingness to shade the truth ("He asked if he could say that on that day I'd held back my natural feelings" [65]), Meursault's honesty seems attractive. Not only this, but Meursault wins the argument about love when he says, "I probably did love Maman, but that didn't mean anything. At one time or another all normal people have wished their loved ones were dead" (65). It is significant that the lawyer has no counter to this point, and any honest reader must accept its validity. The lawyer's anger, his feeling of discomfort in Meursault's presence, results from the appalling possibility that Meursault is indeed, as he claims "just like everybody else," for if this is true then the lawyer has been lying to himself about the love he has for other people (his mother, or his wife perhaps, or his children). Meursault feels the urge to explain himself (but not to apologize) so that the lawyer will no longer feel resentment against him, but he correctly judges that their two positions are irreconcilable and gives up the idea.

Meursault and Religion

Whilst Meursault's defense lawyer is clearly a humanist, a secularist espousing reason, ethics, the social contract, and justice, the examining magistrate is a devout Catholic. This explains why the magistrate is more interested in Meursault himself than in Meursault as a criminal being investigated by the legal system. This is the meaning of his statement, "'What interests me is you,'" although Meursault comments that he did not understand what the magistrate meant at the time (66). It becomes clear that what the magistrate means when he tells Meursault that "with God's help, he would do something for me" is that he hopes to save Meursault's soul; in fact, this is more important to the magistrate than obtaining a conviction in the case (67).

Like the lawyer, the magistrate begins with the issue of whether or not Meursault loved his mother. Once again, Meursault answers with innocent honesty that he loved his mother "'the same as anyone'" (67). As has been pointed out, this is a shocking and indeed frightening answer to anyone who believes that he loves his mother because it challenges that perception and exposes it as self-deception. If Meursault is correct, then every character must see himself in Meursault.

The shocking nature of this truth accounts for the comic reaction of the clerk who is typing out Meursault's answer, "the clerk, who up to then had been typing steadily, must have hit the wrong key because he lost his place and had to go back" (67). The comic effect is heightened by the irony that naively Meursault reports a reaction without any understanding that it has been caused by the shock of his reply.

The magistrate expresses himself perfectly satisfied with Meursault's account of the shooting up to the first shot commenting, "'Fine, fine'" after every sentence. This is because he is able to understand what happened on the beach in rational terms, in terms of the cause and effect with which he is familiar in criminal cases. His sticking point, however, is understanding why, after firing the first shot at the Arab, Meursault paused before firing a further four shots into the body on the ground. This might initially seem to be an important legal question since the answer is relevant to the issue of whether Meursault killed a man in self-defense or in cold blood, but this is not the reason why the magistrate asks the question, or why (faced with Meursault's silence on the matter) he "seemed to be getting fidgety" (67) and repeats the question three times each time with growing desperation and "a strange look on his face" (68). Finally, he demands of Meursault, "'You must tell me,'" and it becomes clear that he needs to know not because of his role as examining magistrate but because the action of firing the four shots, or rather Meursault's failure to explain and to repent of that action, is an offence to his Catholic faith.

For the magistrate, actions must have motives, and motives can be judged on the basis of Catholic ethics: Thou shalt not kill. Meursault, however, is unable to answer the magistrate's question because, as he says, "I didn't know how to answer" (68). This is what he cannot articulate: he shot the man because he had understood that at any moment one may either shoot or not shoot, and because he felt at that moment that it did not matter which of the alternatives he chose. That is to say, he shot the man because he shot the man, an answer which would not satisfy the magistrate's desperate need for a reason for the action even if Meursault could put it into words - which he cannot.

Meursault's failure to answer his question about the pause during the shooting, and his failure to express repentance, threatens the very basis of the magistrate's Catholicism. That is why he reaches for the crucifix and now speaks "in a completely different, almost cracked, voice" which indicates that he has to some degree lost his sanity or at least his rationality (68). The magistrate desperately explains the theology of repentance, but due to the heat, the flies and that fact that the magistrate's frightening demeanor Meursault says that he finds it "very hard to follow his reasoning" (68). The use of the work "reasoning" is clearly intended by Camus to be ironic because reason has nothing to do with what the magistrate is saying; he is speaking of faith, but it is a faith which Meursault does not share. Meursault is about to assure the magistrate that he is "wrong to dwell on it [the pause], because it really didn't matter" (69). It does not matter for Meursault because it is simply what he chose to do, but it matters for the magistrate because the pause means that Meursault must repent in order to save his soul. To the magistrate, it matters in the mind of God; however, not believing in God there is for Meursault there is literally nowhere *for* it to matter.

In fact, the magistrate's desperation is not motivated by the desire to save Meursault's soul so much as it is by his need to save his own fragile faith. With startling honesty, the magistrate tells Meursault that he thinks it is "impossible" that he should not believe in God. He continues that "all men believe in God, even those who turn their backs on him. That was his belief, and if he were ever to doubt it, his life would become meaningless" (69). Meursault's reply is another example of Camus ensuring that his protagonist wins the argument. The magistrate is described as angry and he shouts his question, "'Do you want my life to be meaningless?'" (69). In contrast, Meursault's response is presented as calm, "As far as I could see, it didn't have anything to do with me, and I told him so" (69). Meursault is obviously right: faith is a personal thing, and that faith is no faith at all which depends (like the magistrate's) upon someone else supporting it. Whilst Meursault intends only to deny his complicity in constructing a socio-religious myth of meaning, he unwittingly states a profound truth which he will come to understand only near the end of his life: each person constructs a sense of meaning for him or herself. It is a profound insight, even though Meursault does not at this stage recognize it as such.

The magistrate then loses all restraint and thrusts the crucifix in Meursault's face "screaming irrationally" (69). Meursault's intellectual victory is made crystal clear when, using his normal avoidance strategy, he appears to accept the magistrate's point just to end their interview. The Magistrate's "triumphant" response appears childish, and it is immediately squashed by Meursault's assertion that he will not trust in Christ to save his soul. The narrative presents the magistrate as a pathetically comic character. Showalter concludes, "The portrait of this zealous Christian is rather comic; his excitement, his abrupt gestures, and his non sequiturs make him seem somewhat mad" (53).

The Threat Posed by Meursault

As in his interview with his lawyer, but even more strongly, Meursault emerges as more intellectually honest than the magistrate. The first two representatives of the French judicial system have been ruthlessly satirized by Camus. The two exchanges define the threat that Meursault poses to every other character in the novel, Christian or humanist, since they all (consciously or unconsciously) give meaning to their lives by beliefs (in God, in ethics, in friendship, in love, etc.) which Meursault exposes as illusions because he challenges the validity of those beliefs. Meursault is the little boy in the story "The Emperor's New Clothes" by Hans Christian Andersen who, when the Emperor parades before his subjects in his new clothes, cries out, "But he isn't wearing anything at all!"

It is only by identifying Meursault with the devil and calling him "'Monsieur Antichrist,'" that the magistrate succeeds in explaining away Meursault in terms of Christianity, his own belief system, "The magistrate seemed to have lost interest in me" (70). Once he has done so is able to dismiss Meursault as evil, and once categorized within the magistrate's belief system, Meursault is not longer a threat and the magistrate can once again treat him dismissively with cordial good humor.

To avoid having to defend his decisions, he "made it appear as if I agreed" with the magistrate (69). However, it is significant that when the magistrate presses him with the triumphal cry, "'You see, you see! ... You do believe, don't you, and you're going to place your trust in Him, aren't you?'" Meursault finally says "'no'" (69). This is the voice of dissent: Meursault may not know what he does believe about life, but he is sure that he does not believe in religion. McCarthy makes the same point when he notes, "The novelty of Part 2 is that Meursault's indifference ceases to be instinctive and becomes a reasoned world view" (58). The Meursault who went along with the religious burial of Maman as an alienated stranger has become (at least in that moment) an alienated rebel.

The Sun and the Heat Again

There are four specific interviews referred to in this chapter as well as a series of follow-up interviews which happen over a period of "eleven months" (71). The first two interviews and the follow-ups are relatively stress-free for Meursault, who even remarks of the second that the magistrate is "quite pleasant" (64) and of the later series "I had the ridiculous impression of being 'one of the family'" (70). Significantly, Meursault makes no mention of the heat or the sun in connection with any of these interviews.

The third interview is more demanding, and he notes the "heat" right at the start, though ironically it is his lawyer, in collar and tie and wearing a suit, who seems to suffer more than Meursault who is in shirt sleeves. The final interview is, however, the most stressful, and under pressure Meursault again perceives the sun as hostile. He notes, "It was two o'clock in the afternoon, and this time his office was filled with sunlight barely softened by a flimsy curtain. It was very hot" (66). Remember that Meursault's projection of his psychological discomfort onto the natural world is an avoidance strategy: if the physical world is his enemy, then there is nothing he can do, and he is absolved of responsibility. This is clear when Meursault excuses his failure to understand the magistrate on environmental factors, "To tell the truth, I found it very hard to follow his reasoning, first because it was hot and there were big flies in his office that kept landing on my face, and also because he was scaring me a little" (68). The truth is that Meursault is forced by the magistrate's questions to reflect upon the decisions he has made in his life, and, despite his new assertiveness, Meursault is not yet prepared to do this. Thus, he finds an excuse to avoid self-examination by blaming the heat for his inattention, and as the Magistrate presses him more intensely for answers Meursault reports, "I was getting hotter and hotter" (69).

Summary:

In a number of ways, Part Two is very different from Part One.

Camus is not writing a realistic novel of colonial Algeria.

The focus of the investigation quickly shifts away from the murder of the Arab to Meursault's reaction to the death of his mother.

Camus manipulates the reader to see Meursault as the victim of an arbitrary and invalid process, and to do this the Arab has to disappear.

Meursault is much more assertive and unapologetic about the way he lives his life than at any point in Part One.

In two interviews, the values and beliefs of humanism and Catholicism are subjected to Meursault's criticism and found wanting.

Meursault is forced by the questions of both his defense counsel and the magistrate to reflect upon the way in which he has led his life.

PART TWO Chapter 2: How Experiencing Prison Changes Meursault

'What does it all mean, Mr. Natural?'
'Don't mean sheeeit.' (Robert Crumb)

Consider the following:

1. What is the difference between Meursault's experience of prison before and after his last contact with Marie?

2. What are the physical aspects of confinement that weigh most heavily on Meursault's mind? Explain his comment, "I shouldn't exaggerate ... it was easier for me than for others" (76).

3. What humor does Camus get out of Meursault's delayed understanding of why he is in prison? (See 78)

4. Meursault comments that the story of the Czech murdered by his own mother and sister was "perfectly natural" (80). What does he mean by this? Where has he used this word before in the novel?

5. What was it that the Nurse said at Maman's funeral? Why does Meursault see this statement as relevant to his prison experience? What is he beginning to realize about the events that led up to the murder and the murder itself?

Meursault Provides an Overview

Meursault's narrative has been chronological up to this point, but in this chapter the chronology is disrupted. The chapter begins with one of those few occasions (always clearly indicated) where the narrator uses hindsight, though it is important to note that the narrator is not here using the full understanding of the Meursault at the end of the novel. Rather, the first two paragraphs contrast Meursault's initial feelings about his prison experience, "A few days after I entered prison, I realized that I wouldn't like talking about this part of my life" with how he feels some months later once he has accepted the reality of being locked away from society and the world, "Later on, though, I no longer saw any point to my reluctance" (72). Thus, from the perspective of his attitude once he becomes reconciled to prison, Meursault criticizes his initial failure to grasp the reality of his situation (the same failure which led him to regard his early interrogations as a game), his feeling that "I wasn't really in prison those first few days: I was sort of waiting for something to happen" (72). Meursault precisely identifies the moment when his attitude changes: following her one visit, Marie writes to say that she will be allowed no further visits because she is not his wife. Marie is his last link with society and the natural world, and when he realizes that this link has been cut Meursault begins to accept prison as his new reality.

There are several levels of irony intended by Camus here. Firstly, Marie's letter is yet another instance of decisions having consequences, in this case showing precisely why Meursault's earlier belief that marriage "didn't make any difference to me … didn't really matter" was a ridiculous error (41). Secondly, Camus shows Meursault to be making a profound error when he says, rather self-approvingly, "I felt I was at home in my cell and that my life was coming to a standstill" (72). Meursault is making the mistake of accommodating himself to prison, following his mother's advice to which he refers almost sentimentally, "it was one of Maman's ideas, and she often repeated it, that after a while you could get used to anything" (77). This reminds us of how Salamano got used to the disappointments in his career and his marriage, how Meursault got used to having to give up his studies, how Meursault got used to being Sintés' pal, and how he was going to get used to being married. Getting used to what life throws at you in the belief that "people never change their lives" has been shown in the novel to be an avoidance strategy used by those who have given up on taking responsibility for their lives (41). Meursault is pleased by the idea of withdrawing in his cell from a hostile world and an antagonistic society; it is really only what he has been doing in his apartment since the beginning of the narrative.

The final irony, and the most important for Camus' development of his protagonist and of the ideas that Meursault's development will eventually exemplify, is Meursault's conviction that prison brings his life to a "standstill" (72). This is another ridiculous error. One can see how it is an attractive idea, since each day in prison appears to be "the same unending day that was unfolding in my cell" (80), and "the main problem was killing time" (78). In reality, however, from the moment he enters prison, time is rapidly running out for him - time is killing Meursault. Of course, this has been true from the moment he was born, but entering prison with a trial and execution pending ought to bring this home to Meursault. For the moment, it does not.

Meursault as Naïve Observer

Following his arrest, it takes some time for Meursault to understand the reality of his situation; at first, he is like a man in a dream, a passive observer, strangely dissociated from the things that are happening to him. This is evident in the detailed, matter-of-fact way in which the circumstances of his first days in prison are described. Camus suffuses the narrative with ironic humor (unintentional on Meursault's part) as when he describes his interaction with fellow prisoners, who are predominantly Arabs, "They asked me what I was in for. I said I'd killed an Arab and they were silent. A few minutes later, it got dark. They showed me how to fix the mat I was supposed to sleep on" (72). Meursault perceives without understanding. The short, disjoined sentences convey the narrator's inability to put things together into a coherent whole. It simply does not occur to him that admitting to killing an Arab when he is in a cell where he is the only *pied-noir* surrounded by Arabs places him in real danger given the racially charged atmosphere of Algeria. The reference to the fall of darkness builds tension which is, quite as intentionally on Camus' part, relieved by the comic anti-climax of the Arab prisoners taking almost paternal care of Meursault because of his evident inexperience. Ironically, the Arabs recognize in Meursault a fellow outcast from society: neither they nor he can share the values of colonial Algeria, though for very different reasons. This innocent naiveté disposes the reader to feel sympathy for Meursault.

The Final Contact with Marie

The visit of Marie and the letter that she writes shortly afterwards mark a turning point in Meursault's experience of prison. The interview itself is emotionally demanding (since Marie has feelings for him that Meursault cannot return), and as we expect by now Meursault externalizes the stress he feels into physical discomfort caused by the "sound of the voices echoing off the room's high, bare walls and the harsh light" which makes Meursault feel dizzy and nauseous (73). The reader recognizes the usual excuse for his failure to grasp a situation intellectually and take appropriate action.

The interview with Marie is unsatisfactory despite the pleasure which Meursault takes in seeing a beautiful woman. In contrast to the fluid communication between the Arab prisoners and their visitors, Marie and Meursault have little to say to each other, and their conversation is stilted, conventional, and insincere. The Arabs in the interview room are identical to the people of his neighborhood who Meursault observes from his balcony in Chapter 2: they function effectively and purposefully in their social (in this case family) groups whilst he does not.

Meursault is distracted by what are obviously more successful examples of communication on either side of him. The fat woman and her husband communicate very efficiently using words. The woman in her methodical and pro-active way making arrangements for "him" (74) to be taken care of and "listing all of the things she had put in the basket" which she has left with the guard for her husband reminds the reader of the robotic woman (75). On the other side, the mother and son appear to communicate effectively without words by just "staring at each other" (75). Camus means the reader to contrast the almost telepathic closeness of mother and son here with the gulf which existed between Maman and Meursault in the final years of her life. Together the two Arabs create "an oasis of silence" (75), a beautiful metaphor which recalls Meursault's efforts to reach the spring on the beach, and his complete failure to appreciate his own mother's silence, "When she was at home with me, Maman used to spend her time following me with her eyes, not saying a thing" (5). The distance between Camus and his protagonist is made clear by Camus' expression of his "retrospective gratitude" for the silence of his own family when he wrote, "'Merely by its silence, its reserve, its natural and restrained pride, these people, who could not even read, gave me the highest teaching'" (quoted in Brée *Albert Camus* 5). Significantly, the son says, "'Goodbye Maman'" echoing Meursault's use of the word at the start of the novel (76). These parallel suggests the opportunity which Meursault lost to develop a relationship with his mother.

In contrast with the Arabs, there is no genuine communication between Meursault and Marie (as there was not between Meursault and his lawyer and Meursault and the magistrate). He is aware that her good humor and optimism is a façade adopted for his benefit, that "she was smiling her best smile for me" (74), that it is "forced" (76). Marie urges him to have hope, but he is unsure what she means by the word. The only hope that he can conceive is a return to sensuality, "I wanted to squeeze her shoulders through her dress. I wanted to feel the thin material and I didn't really know what else I had to hope for other than that" (75). He can only speculate that Marie means the same thing that he does. Whatever hope he has is dashed by the letter explaining that, since she is not his wife, Marie will not be allowed to visit him again and by his growing realization that she has moved on with her life.

Sensory Deprivation

As he walks into the visiting room to see Marie, Meursault comments on the negative sense impressions: the shouting voices and the harsh light. In comparison, he says, "My cell was quieter and darker" (73). It seems that, following his meeting with Marie, Meursault gives up on the world and retreats into the womb of his cell, just as he retreated into the "nest" of his apartment in Algiers at the end of Chapter 1 (18). Having made this decision, Meursault reports that during the first few months of his imprisonment "the hardest thing was that my thoughts were still those of a free man" (76). What he misses is defined exclusively in physical terms: going to the beach whenever he wants to, walking down to the sea, "the sound of the first waves under my feet, my body entering the water and the sense of relief it would give me" (76). This marks some intellectual advance: he begins to recognize the significance of things which at the time he took for granted only when he as lost the freedom to experience them.

Prison finally becomes a reality to Meursault, and he begins the painful process by which (like a drug addict) he is weaned off of his dependence on pleasurable sensation. The first loss that he feels is sex, and he comments that he "was tormented by my desire for a woman" (77). It is significant that he does not here name Marie; it is the physical aspect of sexuality rather than the emotional aspect that Meursault misses, and he compensates by fantasies and memories in which Marie has no more significant role than do any of the other women Meursault has "enjoyed" – a word which implies that they meant nothing more to him than pure self-gratification (77).

When he naively complains to the guard that this treatment is "unfair," the guard explains that not being able to have contact with women is part the punishment, "'They've taken away your freedom,'" and Meursault, after reflecting that he has "never thought about that" before, agrees (78). This is the first instance in the novel where Meursault, a man not given to reflection on his relationship with the world, is forced to evaluate his present existence and to contrast it to his former life – more intellectual progress. Ironically, the loss of freedom of choice through imprisonment will eventually lead Meursault to understand the importance of choice, for what the guard says here is actually the reverse of the truth: in his years as a free man, sensuality was used by Meursault as an *alternative* to action, as a way of evading the absurd. In so far as it constituted revolt, it was self-destructive, a way of passing time rather than of experiencing time. Meursault's addiction to cigarettes illustrates this point, but it is significant how completely (though not easily) this addiction is broken. He comments that he eventually got "used to not smoking and it wasn't a punishment anymore" (78), and it is significant that when he is offered a cigarette before the opening of his trial, he refuses (82).

During the painful period of withdrawal, when Meursault indulges in vicarious sense impressions as a substitute for both sex and smoking, he takes refuge in sleep as he always has during times of stress. He becomes so good at this that eventually he leaves himself with only six hours each day "to kill" (79). The use of this phrase indicates how far Meursault still is from achieving authentic existence, for as Camus states in *The Myth of Sisyphus*, "The absurd man is he who is not apart from time" (72). Meursault is so apart from time that he feels its slow passage to be his enemy, something to be got through rather than something to be experienced.

Meursault and Time

For Meursault, being in prison creates the illusion of timelessness, and his response to this illusion is passivity. He plays a memory game, building up a more and more detailed mental picture of his apartment room, a detailed inventory of "things" including the "color and texture" of each "flake … crack, or … chipped edge" (79). Once again, the limitation of this strategy is that it focuses exclusively on sense impressions.

Time passes (though he loses track of its passing), and he feels his life come to a standstill because, "For me it was one and the same unending day that was unfolding in my cell" (80). This is a dangerous viewpoint because it ignores time as progression towards death, and by denying mortality it avoids confrontation with the absurd. The absurd man must situate himself in time (*Myth* 13).

The Newspaper Story

Another diversion is the newspaper story about a murder in Czechoslovakia which Meursault reads and meditates upon constantly. (Improbable as it may seem, the story is actually based on an Associated Press story published in the Algerian newspapers in January, 1935 [Lottman 85]. Camus would later use the article as the basis for his play *The Misunderstanding* produced in 1944.) Meursault concludes firstly, that the story is unlikely (presumably because the artificial plot development makes it seem too much like a morality tale), but secondly, and somewhat contradictorily, that the motivations in the story are "perfectly natural ... [and that] the traveler pretty much deserved what he got and that you should never play games" (80). Implicitly, Meursault here acknowledges that decisions have consequences, which marks a complete reversal of his earlier views and a significant development in his understanding of life. However, he is still not factoring morality into this understanding. Meursault uses the word "naturally" in Chapter 2 when he misunderstands his boss's apparent annoyance at his asking for two days off to attend his mother's funeral, "naturally my boss thought about the fact that I'd be getting four days' vacation that way" (19). What unites his judgments of his boss and of the mother and daughter is Meursault's tendency to assume that people are motivated only by self-interest, an assumption he makes because he understands neither emotional nor ethical motivation. In both cases, Meursault misjudges. In the case of newspaper story, it is the murder which is the crime rather than the (ill-advised) deception practiced by the victim. Meursault has yet to understand that, although at any moment one may either shoot or not shoot, the truth that "'Everything is permitted' ... does not recommend crime, for this would be childish" (*Myth* 67). Meursault's consciousness remains at the level of a child

The Beginning of Self-Knowledge

The chapter ends, however, with a significant development. The man who almost boasted that he "had pretty much lost the habit of analyzing myself" spends a long time looking at his reflection in his tin plate (65). He notes that he seems to have no control over the image which he sees, "I smiled and it still had the same sad, stern expression" (76). What he sees, reflected in a plate which is provided by the prison system, an arm of the state, is 'Meursault' as defined by society: he sees Meursault the prisoner, an image over which he has no control because it is an identity defined by society. At precisely the same moment, however, he also realizes that he can hear the sound of his own voice, a sound which has "been ringing in my ears for many long days ... all the time I had been talking to myself" (76). Meursault literally finds his own voice at this point, a voice different from that of society, a voice of dissent. This is the key to understanding his true identity, an identity which he does control.

It is significant that this happens in the evenings when the day is dying. Meursault refers to the "cortege of silence" which marks "the last light of day" (81). The nights prove that he is not living an "unending day"; the nights bring him back to an understanding of the passage of time, and (although he is not at the time aware of this) this is why he is reminded at this moment of "what the nurse at Maman's funeral said. No, there was no way out, and no one can imagine what nights in prison are like" (81). Meursault is just beginning to confront the absurd reality of human life, and he is able to do this, despite his nature which is not self-reflective, because prison provides a context where he does not have the distractions of either society or the natural world. Intellectually, he is making progress which is what McCarthy means when he comments that this chapter "depicts Meursault's evolution during his months in prison and traces a growth in his awareness that prepares us for his attitude during the trial" (57).

Summary:

This chapter is written from the perspective of Meursault at the end of the chapter not that of the Meursault at the end of the novel.

Meursault appears more sympathetic because of his child-like inability to understand the situations he is in.

The interview with Marie is a failure in a room full of people who communicate successfully.

One important effect of prison is to wean Meursault off his addiction to sensual gratification.

Becoming reconciled to the reality of prison is not the positive development which Meursault as narrator presents it as being.

Meursault is, almost despite himself, becoming more self-aware, but until he faces the reality of his imminent death he is evading the human situation.

.

PART TWO Chapter 3: The Trial

Death destroys a man, but the idea of death saves him. (E. M. Forster *Howards End*)

Consider the following:

1. Before the trial starts, what evidence is there that Meursault totally underestimates the seriousness of his situation? Meursault's comments indicate that he feels himself to be a detached observer rather than a person on trial for their life. Which of his comments give you this impression?

2. Comment on the unconscious irony of Meursault's reaction to being asked his name, age, date of birth, etc., "I realized it was only natural, because it would be a very serious thing to try the wrong man" (87).

3. What rational explanation of Meursault's crime is offered by the prosecution and how does the testimony of the witnesses add support to it?

4. How does Meursault's perception of himself in relation to the trial change as the case proceeds, and it becomes increasingly clear that he will be found guilty? Comment particularly on his statements:

a) "I had this stupid urge to cry because I could feel how much all these people hated me" (90);

b) "I felt a stirring go through the room and for the first time I realized that I was guilty" (90);

c) "... it was the first time in my life I ever wanted to kiss a man" (93).

[The following comment from Spark Notes seems to be very helpful: "Meursault comes to understand that his failure to interpret or find meaning in his own life has left him vulnerable to others, who will impose such meaning for him. Until this point, Meursault has unthinkingly drifted from moment to moment, lacking the motivation or ability to examine his life as a narrative with a past, present, and future. Even during the early part of trial he watches as if everything were happening to someone else. Only well into the trial does Meursault suddenly realize that the prosecutor has successfully manufactured an interpretation of Meursault's life, and that, in the jury's eyes, he likely appears guilty."]

5. What does Meursault's lawyer mean when he says of the trial, "'everything is true and nothing is true!'" (91).

6. Comment on Meursault's closing statement, "No, there was no way out, and no one can imagine what nights in prison are like" (81).

The Trial as Allegory and as Realism

The description of the trial of Meursault is an uneasy, some would say an unsatisfactory, combination of realism and allegory. Just as Camus utilizes certain realistic elements of his Algerian setting and disregards others, so in describing the trial he gives the impression of strict realism whilst ultimately writing allegory. Brian Fitch places this chapter in context in a way that explains Camus' intentions:

> The whole of the second part of *L'Etranger* ... proposes a number of interpretations or reconstitutions of the preceding part ... [T]he reader is convinced of the inaccuracy of a given interpretation (that of the examining magistrate, Meursault's lawyer, or the prosecuting counsel, for example) *not* because it departs from any of the other interpretations proposed since all they have in common is their fictive status as *a posteriori* fabrications, but rather because of the heavy irony that pervades all the scenes involving the confrontation between Meursault and the various

representatives of the legal system" (quoted in Bloom ed. 61-2 original emphasis).

The trial sequence represents society's attempt to maintain rational order. Brée describes the official characters who Meursault encounters in Part Two as "little more than subtly wrought masks incarnating and deliberately satirizing interpretations that Camus rejects as irrelevant – guilt, remorse, atonement, conversion" (*Albert Camus* 18). The prosecutor and Meursault's lawyer each offer interpretations of Meursault's crime that are based on logic, reason, morality, psychology, and (above all) the concept of cause and effect. However, these interpretations have no basis in fact and serve only as attempts to obscure the frightening idea that life is ultimately irrational. McCarthy asserts that, "*The Stranger* strips the legal system and the French State of their legitimacy" (2). The entire trial is absurd - a futile attempt to impose order on a disordered world.

At this point in the novel, Camus might have presented Meursault's condemnation by the French Judicial System in the surreal allegorical terms used by Kafka to describe Joseph K's confrontation with the inaccessible authorities of the state in *The Trial* or K. the Land-Surveyor's efforts to overcome bureaucracy in *The Castle*. However, Camus draws on his experience as a reporter on trials for the *Alger Républicain* in 1938 and 1939 to keep the description of the legal procedure of Meursault's trial grounded in realism. (English and American readers need to take into account the very different nature of the French trial system.) As Brée comments, "unlike the nightmarish world of Kafka, the world of Meursault is a brilliantly lighted, clearly delineated, everyday world, that of Algiers" (*Albert Camus* 15), Nevertheless, the trial develops in a way which is far from realistic; Gay-Crosier calls it a "semi believable account of a murder trial as it might have been conducted in a French court of the 1930s' (76). Showalter describes the trial as frankly implausible. He cites as evidence that the policeman who arrested Meursault and investigated the crime is not called and neither is the second Arab, that Masson gives no testimony about the first confrontation with the Arabs, that Sintès gives no details of being cut by the Arab's knife, and that Marie is not asked about seeing the Arabs that morning (48-9). As has been pointed out, the crime of shooting an Arab is hardly mentioned; Meursault is tried by society for having a world view which threatens the very foundations of Catholicism and society. Ultimately, his crime is that he is "a monster, a man without morals" (96).

Meursault as Naïve Narrator

As at the beginning of the first two chapters in Part Two, Meursault seems not to understand the significance of the process in which he is caught up. When he hears chairs being dragged across the floor, he makes an inappropriate association with "those neighborhood fêtes when the hall is cleared for dancing after the concert," unconsciously referencing a life which, although he appears not to have realized it, he has lost forever (82). Asked by a policeman if he is nervous, he replies that he is not "and that, in a way, I was even interested to see a trial. I'd never had the chance before" (83). Meursault simply does not associate himself with the criminal that society defines him as being. This is why, when he identifies the jury, he has the impression that they are like people on a tram giving a new passenger the once-over "to see if they could find something funny about him" (83). Even Meursault recognizes that this association is inappropriate, but it seems that he can only grasp the fact that he is being put on trial for his life in the abstract. It is not to him a reality, "I knew it was a silly idea since it wasn't anything funny they were after but a crime" (83). Even this attempt to bring himself back to reality is significant because it concentrates on the jury and the crime, but makes no mention of the accused. Finally, Meursault comments that "There isn't much difference" between being judged by a jury and by fellow passengers on a tram, which marks a reversion to the kind of valueless thinking which Meursault used throughout Part One, which the novel has shown to be an evasion, and which he has begun to move beyond in the year since his arrest.

Meursault admits that "at first I hadn't realized that all those people were crowding in to see me. Usually people didn't pay much attention to me. It took some doing on my part to understand that I was the cause of all the excitement" (83). Notice again, that there is no reference by Meursault to the crime with which he is charged. Camus' aim is to gain sympathy for his protagonist by making him seem to be a victim which can only be done, of course, by ignoring the actual victim in the case.

The Gentlemen of the Press and the Officers of the Court

Another way in which Camus gains sympathy for Meursault is by presenting those around him in an unattractive light. McCarthy goes so far as to say that Camus "satirizes the reporters" (59). The reporters do indeed appear to treat Meursault's case as entertainment. One admits lightly that they have inflated their reporting of Meursault's case (and of the case which will follow it) because, "'Summer is the slow month for the news'" (84), and they "joked and laughed together completely at ease" despite the serious nature of the charge and its implications for the accused (85). Meursault comments that "all had the same indifferent and somewhat snide look on their faces," and Camus here taps into the anti-Paris motif that runs through the novel describing the most unattractive reporter as a "special correspondent for a Paris paper" (84).

The reporters superciliously look down on Meursault whilst pretending affability and are, as we have already seen, perfectly prepared to distort the truth to give their reporting more impact. Meursault's immediate impression is that they form a group from which he is excluded, "everyone was waving and exchanging greetings and talking, as if they were in a club where people are glad to find themselves among others from the same world. That is how I explained to myself the strange impression I had of being odd man out, a kind of intruder" (84). In this description, the reader sees Meursault's relationship with the reporters as a microcosm of his relationship with society as a whole. The reporters represent society in that they explain things; for the reporters the world is governed by rules which they all understand. That is why they form a "club" to which Meursault is a stranger.

One reporter, however, stands out. He is different from the others in that he is "much younger than the others," and "he had left his pen lying in front of him and was looking at me … his two very bright eyes … were examining me closely without betraying any definable emotion. And I had the odd impression of being watched by myself" (85). Unlike the others, who have already come to an understanding of Meursault, this reporter is simply studying him. Olivier Todd identifies this encounter between protagonist and journalist as "an Alfred Hitchcock-like appearance in his own work" (78). Camus enters the narrative here to suggest an alternative to the court's way of looking at Meursault which is, of course, the way in which he is presented in the novel.

The description of the lawyers and the three judges stresses the colors black and red, both of which are associated in the novel with death ("the screws on the casket had been tightened … there were four men wearing black" [14]; "the blood-red earth spilling over Maman's casket" [18]). The men themselves appear grotesquely comic, the prosecutor being tall and thin and wearing pince-nez and the senior judge having a "little bald head" (85).

The Testimony of the Witnesses

The actual crime for which Meursault is on trial, the shooting of an Arab, is referred to only twice in this chapter. At the start of his examination, the chief judge re-reads "the narrative of what I'd done" and asks Meursault to confirm its accuracy, which he does (87). The prosecutor asks whether, armed with the gun, he returned to the spring with the intention of killing the Arab, and Meursault denies it saying that "it just happened that way" (88). Meursault 's reply defines the essential difference between Meursault and everyone else in the courtroom; they operate in a world given order and meaning by rules and shared codes of behavior, whereas he implicitly asserts that the world is in fact random. The shock of his assertion accounts for the "nasty voice" in which the prosecutor says, "'That will be all for now'" (88). This is the only reference to the Arab until the conclusion of the witness testimony; the examination turns to what the judge describes as "some questions that might seem irrelevant to my case but might in fact have a significant bearing on it" (87). Meursault is effectively being tried by society for being a stranger in Part One.

The questioning of the director brings out a number of ways in which Meursault broke the rules of society: he put his mother in a home; he was calm and did not cry at her funeral; he left immediately after the funeral without paying his "last respects to her grave"; and he did not know his mother's age (89). Having succeeded in bringing out these points, the prosecutor concludes "with such glee and with such a triumphant look in my direction that for the first time in years I had the stupid urge to cry, because I could feel how much all these people hated me" (89-90). The reader is reminded of all of those times in Part One when Meursault felt guilty about having said or done the wrong thing, felt vaguely that the rest of society was playing a game the rules of which he did not understand. Now that society is literally ranged against him, it inevitably makes him feel that he is indeed the guilty one.

The testimony of the caretaker adds to the list of social norms which Meursault has violated: he did not wish to see his mother's body, and he smoked, slept and drank coffee during the vigil. The attempts of Meursault's lawyer to defend him fail. When he argues that the caretaker also smoked, the man replies, "'I know I was wrong to do it,'" which again marks the difference between Meursault and everyone else in the courtroom because he does not think that what he did was wrong (90). When the caretaker points out that it was he who offered Meursault the coffee, the prosecutor says, "'a stranger may offer a cup of coffee, but ... beside the body of the one who brought him into the world, a son should have refused it'" (91). Once again, as with the caretaker's statement above, this is an argument based on shared moral values. The words "wrong" and "should" are, however, without meaning to Meursault.

Pérez testifies that he did not see Meursault cry at the funeral and Cèleste that Meursault speaks little and does not always pay off his bill regularly. Before he leaves, Cèleste tries desperately to say something which will aid Meursault's defense, but the best he can say is that it was "bad luck" (92). As he goes out, he shows his frustration at his failure, and Meursault comments that, "it was the first time in my life I ever wanted to kiss a man" (93). This is very significant in Meursault's development because it is the first time that he acknowledges that friendship has genuine meaning and feels the urge to respond with friendship. This is very different from his indifferent response to Sintès' desire to be his pal or to Marie's offer of love and marriage.

When questioned, Marie is forced to add to the list of ways in which Meursault has acted anti-socially: the day after his mother's death he went swimming, started a '"dubious liaison,'" and went to watch a comedy film (94). In Meursault's defense, Marie claims, sobbing, that "it wasn't like that, there was more to it," but the reader knows that for Meursault there was nothing more to his relationship with Marie than physical pleasure (94). Masson and Salamano testify, the latter confirming that Meursault "had run out of things to say to" his mother and had therefore "put her in a home" (94). Again, Meursault looks out on society en masse and finds that "no one seemed to understand," confirming his status as a stranger to the shared values of society (95).

The testimony of Sintès is probably the most damning to Meursault because it is clear to everyone in the courtroom that he is a vicious criminal, something which Meursault has failed to understand. Sintès admits that Meursault wrote "the letter that set the whole drama in motion," did not intervene when the girl was being beaten, and testified on his behalf at the police station (95). The prosecutor concludes that Meursault is, in fact, his "accomplice" in criminal acts (95), "a monster, a man without morals," and finally draws the elements of his case together, "'[a] man who the day after his mother died was indulging in the most shameful debauchery killed a man for the most trivial of reasons and did so in order to settle an affair of unspeakable vice'" (96). What the prosecutor is asserting here is a pattern of moral corruption against which Meursault could only offer (assuming that he could articulate his ideas, which he cannot) the view that his life has been a series of random and meaningless decisions. Society sees Meursault's indifference at his mother's death as the same crime as killing the Arab because both offend against society's most cherished values. This is why the prosecutor concludes, "'I accuse this man of burying his mother with crime in his heart!'" (96). Meursault notes the strong impact which this statement has on the people who are there to judge him and realizes that "things weren't going well for me" (96). The reader finds this an unconsciously comic understatement.

Meursault Analyzes Himself

Just as the previous chapter concludes with profound introspection, so too does this. Sitting in the "the darkness of my mobile prison," Meursault, driven in the back of a van from the courtroom to the prison, experiences the sound, smell and feel of a summer evening in Algiers (97). It is his loss of these things which leads Meursault to understand their value, "the familiar sounds of a town I had loved and of a certain time of day when I used to feel happy" (97). Earlier in the courtroom, Meursault comes close to expressing love for Cèleste, but now he actually uses the word "love," a word which he had earlier said "didn't mean anything," for the first time in the narrative (41). Only now, when it is no longer possible, does Meursault realize that "it was an hour when, a long time ago, I was perfectly content" (97). The trial has forced Meursault to define himself in opposition to the power of the state and now, for the first time he admits to feeling love and implicitly acknowledges the value of happiness and contentment.

Meursault's self-analysis has momentarily taken him beyond a simple re-assertion of the world view which he lived by in Part One. However, at this crucial moment he reverts to the error of that world view by regarding man as helpless, "familiar paths traced in summer skies could lead as easily to prison as to the sleep of the innocent" (97). What Meursault has not yet understood is that love, happiness, and contentment are not accidents which happen along the route to the grave; our lives are not "mapped out" for us (97).

Summary:

Although the procedures of the trial are realistically presented, the way in which the focus is shifted to an examination of the way Meursault has lived his life in Part One is allegory not realism;

Camus' essential criticism of the trial is that the plausible interpretations which are imposed onto Meursault's conduct in Part One are palpably false.

By the end of this chapter, Meursault has understood that love, happiness and contentment can give life value; he has still not yet understood that man's freedom to choose how to live his life is actually meaningful.

PART TWO Chapter 4: Society's Verdict

> What does nihilism mean? That the higher values
> are losing their value. The ends are lacking, there is
> no answer to this question 'What's the use?'
> (Friedrich Nietzsche *Will To Power* aphorism 2)

Consider the following:

1. What does Meursault find interesting about hearing people talk about himself? Why does hearing them lead to a return of his feeling of disengagement from the court proceedings ("they seemed to be arguing the case as if it had nothing to do with me" [98])?

2. What does he find "plausible" and consistent in the prosecution's account of his actions?

3. How does the prosecution succeed in linking Meursault's case to the parricide case that will follow this trial?

4. How does Meursault respond to his lawyer's use of first person narrative to present Meursault's motives to the jury?

5. At the start of the chapter, Meursault asks, "were the two speeches [those of the prosecution and the defense] so different after all?" (98). What do they have in common in relation to Meursault?

6. What is unusual, as compared with most defendants, about Meursault's reaction to his lawyer's explanation that there is very little chance of "overturning the verdict" (106)?

7. Show how, near the end of both Chapters 3 and 4, Meursault becomes aware of the life-experiences that he has lost as a result of his actions. Comment on the irony of this realization.

Meursault's Total Alienation

This chapter contains the summations of the prosecutor and defender and the verdict. Inevitably, there is a good deal of repetition since the summations refer to testimony already given in the previous chapter which in turn refers to incidents described in Part One. Camus uses the trial as a device for allowing society to pass its verdict on the way in which Meursault has lived his life. Meursault recognizes what is at stake when he comments that "there was a lot said about me, maybe more about me than about my crime" (98). The murder of the Arab is seen as a logical extension of a life lived without the values and emotions which underpin civilized society. Meursault retains his naiveté throughout the chapter concentrating exclusively on what is said and appearing still not to have grasped that his life hangs in the balance. However, the naiveté is expressed overtly only in the first, unintentionally comic, sentence, "Even in the prisoner's dock it's always interesting to hear people talk about you" (98).

Meursault only finds it interesting to hear what others say about him only for a short while, however, because he is soon alienated by the fact that he is given no role in his own defense. Initially, Meursault fights against the urge to speak out in court realizing that, "I didn't have anything to say" (98). Although he knows that what the lawyers are saying about him is pure invention, Meursault has no alternative explanation for shooting the Arab because he has no understanding of it. This becomes clear when, having listened to the whole of the prosecutor's speech, Meursault accepts the invitation of the judge to address the court, "I said, almost at random, in fact, that I never intended to kill the Arab … Fumbling a little with my words and realizing how ridiculous I sounded, I blurted out that it was because of the sun. People laughed" (102-3). The words "at random" and "blurted" indicate that, whilst Meursault rejects the analytical framework used by the lawyers to argue that he is or is not a man who deserves to be executed for his crime, he has no analytical framework to put in its place; that is, he has still not understood why he did what he did. In fact, absent this understanding, Meursault's account of the crime *is* laughable – to kill a man "because of the sun" – suggesting that he had no free will in the decision, no intention to kill, no responsibility for the killing.

The truth (which is reflected in the narrator's retrospective commentary on the shooting at the end of Part One) is that Meursault shoots the Arab because he misunderstands man's relationship with the sun and hence with the world, an explanation which the officials and the public in the court would certainly find equally laughable could Meursault have put it into words - which he cannot. Bloom comments that, "For an intelligent man, he does not seem to have grasped how he could best work within the system" (Bloom ed. 47). This is, of course, Camus' entire point and the theme of the chapter: Meursault cannot work *within* the legal system because it embodies and ultimately enforces values to which he is a stranger.

Opposing World Views

As his trial progresses, Meursault comes to understand that his own failure to interpret or find meaning in his own life has left him vulnerable to those who will impose a meaning which is based upon entirely false assumptions but which sounds plausible, even to Meursault himself. Thus, Meursault asks of the summations by the prosecutor and his own defense lawyer, "were the two speeches so different after all?" (98). The question is rhetorical since the speeches patently use the same conceptual framework and differ only in the conclusions which they draw.

The prosecutor first blackens Meursault's character by alluding to his uncertainty about his mother's age, his flirting with Marie, his attending a comedy film with her, and finally his sleeping with her to establish that Meursault has a "criminal soul" (98). Secondly, the prosecutor describes Meursault's criminal connection with Sintès in such a way as to make the shooting of the Arab appear to be both deliberate and premeditated. Listening to him, Meursault comments, almost admiringly, "I thought his way of viewing the events had a certain consistency. What he was saying was plausible" (98). The prosecutor has succeeded, in Meursault's eyes, in making sense out of an action which he himself cannot explain – all that Meursault and the reader know is that, however plausible it sounds, this is *not* how it happened.

The prosecutor continues by arguing that Meursault's lack of remorse is yet another indication of his having killed the Arab "with full knowledge of his actions" (99). Once again, Meursault is forced to admit the justice of what the prosecutor is saying, "I couldn't help admitting that he was right. I didn't feel much remorse for what I had done" (99). Meursault's own explanation, that he has "never been able to truly feel remorse for anything" because he has concentrated throughout his life on the immediate future and never looked back at the past, shows that he is still convinced that one choice is equivalent to another. The prosecutor's conclusion is that "nothing human, not one of the principles that govern men's hearts, was within my reach" (101), whilst Meursault knows that he has no time for principles simply because principles are false – in a world where events are entirely random and meaningless, principles are a fraud. However, as clearly as Meursault knows this, he also knows that "given the position I was in, I couldn't talk to anyone in that way" because they simply dare not accept that conception of the world and of man's place in it (100).

In his summation, the prosecutor presents Meursault as "a monster" who has no place in society because he ignores its "fundamental rules" (102). Meursault is described as having "not one of the moral principles that govern men's hearts," and, being such, his very existence is seen as a threat to society (101). The prosecutor establishes a motivational chain of causality, beginning with Meursault's insensitivity to his mother's death and ending with the firing of four shots at point blank range, which he uses to conclude that the killing was "premeditated" (98). Camus is here showing how essential it is for society to be able to explain Meursault's action, but the explanation is absurd. Ironically, Meursault comes close to understanding this when he comments that the explanation of his actions "had a certain consistency ... was plausible" (99). The narrative in Part Once has, however, made it clear that Meursault does not act consistently, each decision being taken separately and without any understanding of its possible connection to other decisions: Meursault effectively sleepwalks through life in Part One.

The ultimate absurdity of the prosecutor's argument is his assertion that Meursault is "morally guilty of killing his mother" (101-2). This makes it clear that Meursault's crime is lack of moral values and the emotions which they generate. He is guilty of feeling no remorse for the death either of his mother *or* of the Arab, and Meursault has to admit that this is true, "Of course, I couldn't help admitting that he was right. I didn't feel much remorse for what I had done" (100). Unable to present an alternative explanation of his actions, Meursault has little alternative but to see himself as a "monster" (102).

Like the prosecutor, the defense lawyer seeks to impose a pattern on Meursault's experience, and in this sense "defense and prosecution agree: demonstrating that the conflict is never between them but between Meursault and the entire court" (McCarthy 62). However, whilst the prosecutor is able to describe a pattern which Meursault finds "plausible" (99), his "less talented" (103) lawyer fails in Meursault's view. The entire endeavor alienates Meursault who, being aware that there is no pattern, cannot relate to what either man is saying. In the case of his own lawyer, this alienation is accentuated by the fact that the lawyer uses the first person when describing Meursault's actions, causing Meursault to feel "completely taken aback ... I thought it was a way to exclude me even further from the case" (103). In effect, the defense lawyer's summation echoes the views of the director of the home at Marengo that Meursault does not have to "'justify'" (4) his decision to place his mother in the home, and the view of his boss by describing Meursault as a "'tireless worker, loyal to the firm'" (104). However, Meursault notices two weaknesses in

156

the summation. Firstly, his lawyer rushes through an argument that Meursault was provoked into shooting the Arab, since for him (as for the prosecutor) it is Meursault's "soul" which is on trial (103), and secondly he makes no mention of Meursault's conduct at the funeral, because Meursault has given him nothing with which to defend or even explain his lack of emotion.

Meursault's Growing Self Awareness

Meursault's attention wanders from his lawyer's speech to the sounds of the world outside. The sound of an ice cream seller's horn reminds him of "a life that wasn't mine anymore" (104). Aware of this loss, for the first time in the novel, Meursault truly appreciates that he lived his life a world in which he achieved happiness, "one in which I'd found the simplest and most lasting joys: the smells of summer, the part of town I loved, a certain evening sky, Marie's dresses and the way she laughed" (104). (Compare, "the familiar sounds of a town I had loved" [97].) What is familiar here is that Meursault's happiness is linked exclusively to pleasant sensations, but what is new is the importance which his language gives to the experience of pleasant sensations. He says that they produce "*lasting* joys," (emphasis added) implying that the memory of happiness is able to sustain a person through times of unhappiness; he who has denied the emotion of human love uses precisely that word to describe his experience of parts of Algiers. Even as he is awaiting the verdict, Meursault is able to sense "the sweetness of the evening coming on" (105), another sign that happiness is possible in life no matter how adverse the circumstances of life.

It is significant that Camus wrote Part Two of the novel in 1940 while living in Paris and working on the newspaper *Paris-Soir*, when he (like Meursault) felt himself to be in exile from the life of the *pied-noir* which he had lived in Algeria. Olivier Todd refers to a letter written in May to his future wife Francine in which Camus wrote that "his book [*The Stranger*] reminded him of his exile and of the kingdom on the other side of the Mediterranean: 'I think of a sentence from my novel: "Over there, over there too, evening is like a melancholy respite."' He thought of evenings in Algiers and Oran: 'How much I would like that respite by the sea'" (Todd 110).

Thus, Camus shared Meursault's tender memories, but the essential difference is that whilst Camus knew that he could eventually return to Algeria, Meursault knows that he is thinking about a life which he has lost forever. It is as though this brief glimpse of having feelings is much too overwhelming for Meursault. His memories make what he is doing in the court appear to be "utter pointlessness" and he wishes "to get it over with and get back to my cell and sleep" (105). On one level, he is right: what is happening in the court is based on absurd assumptions about life and is, frankly, a farce. However, on another level, Meursault is still terribly wrong. Firstly, as pointless as it may seem, what happens in the court is a matter of life and death to him – something he still does not appear to have grasped. Secondly, and more importantly, returning to the womb of his cell and seeking refuge from life in unconsciousness is just as absurd – giving up on life and on happiness is no answer to human mortality.

The Verdict

In contrast to his interest in the world outside the courtroom, Meursault is over-whelmed by the "utter pointlessness" the legal proceedings (105). Even his friends like Celeste, Raymond and Marie have no meaning for him. He justifies not even having looked at Marie throughout the entire trial with the patent falsehood that "I'd just had too much to do," though he is finally honest with himself about his inability to return her "worried little smile" admitting that his "heart felt nothing" (105).

Meursault's impassive reaction to the verdict is an extension of his alienation from the proceedings of the trial; if one feels that the person being discussed is not oneself then one can have no emotional engagement with the verdict. Beyond, his lack of emotion, Meursault's reaction to this part of the legal process is contradictory. When his lawyer explains that he has not filed any motions during the trial which could be the basis for an appeal because appeals are seldom granted, this strikes Meursault as logical. Since Meursault has not associated the verdict with the possibility of his own ceasing to exist, the efficient shipping clerk in him is able to view the appeals process "objectively," appreciating that appeals must be kept to a minimum, "Otherwise there would be too much pointless paperwork" (106). In contrast, Meursault finds the process by which the verdict and sentence are presented to be ridiculous. It culminates with the judge stating "in bizarre language that I was to have my head cut off in a public square in the name of the French people" (107). Using the language of dissent more fluently than at any other time in the novel, Meursault mocks the judge's complex and arcane language ("in the name of the French people") by stating the verdict in words of one syllable ("I was to have my head cut off") bringing home the stark reality of the verdict which is precisely what the judge's legalese is designed to obscure. The simplicity of Meursault's language actually emphasizes the absurdity of such a barbaric action being taken in the name of the people, an abstract concept which has no meaning for Meursault and which, because the first four chapters of Part Two have manipulated the reader into identifying sympathetically with Meursault, have no meaning for the reader. It is significant that Camus was himself a life-long opponent of capital punishment.

By the end of this chapter, Camus has successfully established Meursault "as the man who lives honestly and who is victimized by an oppressive, falsely humanistic society" (McCarthy 66). What remain is for Camus to answer the question of whether a life which will end in total negation can have any value at all.

Summary:

The legal system finds Meursault to be a "monster" (102), but this chapter subjects that system to withering satire.

In their summations the prosecutor and the defender each construct a false identity for Meursault.

Meursault himself feels entirely excluded from the trial, but given an opportunity to speak he can offer no explanation for the way he has lived his life.

Meursault finds the prosecutor's argument "plausible" (99) and "right" (100).

Meursault develops a conscious and intense appreciation for the "lasting joys" of a life which he has now lost forever (104).

Meursault still does not grasp the real consequences of a guilty verdict.

PART TWO Chapter 5: Temptation and Triumph

> Depend upon it, sir, when a man knows he is to be hanged in a fortnight, it concentrates his mind wonderfully. (Boswell *Life of Samuel Johnson*).

Consider the following

1. At the start of this chapter, Meursault says, "All I care about right now is escaping the machinery of justice, seeing if there's any way out of the inevitable" (108). How has his attitude changed since his trial?

2. What does Meursault mean when he says that "there really was something out of proportion between the verdict such certainty was based on and the imperturbable march of events from the moment the verdict was announced" (109)?

3. In what ways is hope a barrier that Meursault must overcome before he can come to terms with his situation?

4. By what difficult (but accurate) reasoning does Meursault persuade himself finally "to accept [the idea] of the rejection of my appeal" (114)?

5. How does the chaplain give meaning to his life? How does Meursault react to the philosophy (or theology) that the chaplain urges him to accept?

6. Following his confrontation with the chaplain, Meursault experiences an epiphany, "I was sure about me, about everything ... sure of my life and sure of the death I had waiting me ... I had been right, I was still right, I was always right" (120-1). He gets it! Understanding this epiphany is the key to understanding Camus' message, his purpose in writing the book, and his absurdist philosophy. (Camus always rejected the label 'existentialist,' but critics have continued to apply it to his thinking.)

a) Meursault goes on to ask repeatedly the rhetorical question, "What did it matter...?" (121) Explain why none of the things that he considers matters.

b) What does Meursault mean when he says, "Everyone was privileged. There were only privileged people" (121)? (We are not just privileged because we have been born and so given a life.)

c) What does he mean when he refers to the chaplain as "this condemned man" (122)? Why is his use of this word ironic?

7. Look carefully at the final paragraph of the novel:

a) Now that Meursault has accepted that, "Nothing, nothing mattered" (121), how does he react to the physical beauties of the world he is about to leave?

b) How does he explain his mother's taking a "fiancé" at the end of her life?

c) What does he mean when he says of his mother, "Nobody, nobody had the right to cry over her" (122)?

d) What does he mean by the oxymoron "the gentle indifference of the world ... so like a brother, really" (emphasis added 122-3)?

e) Why does he want to die with "a large crowd of spectators ... [who will] greet me with cries of hate" (123)?

8. Spark Notes make the comment that at the end of the novel Meursault comes to understand "the redemptive value of abandoning hope." Comment on the meaning of this paradox.

The Relationship of Narrator and Author

First person narrative always raises the question of the relationship of narrator and author. The Meursault of Part One is clearly distinct from the author, but just as clearly the gap narrows as Part Two progresses, so that it is tempting to believe that the two become one at the end of the novel. That this is not true is clear from one of Camus' earliest notes on the theme of the novel in his journal of April 1937, "Narrative – the man who does not want to explain himself. He dies, alone in being conscious of his truth – Vanity of this consolation" (quoted in Lottman 136). It is significant here that Camus refers to the truth which Meursault finds as "his" rather than 'the' truth, and that he terms Meursault's sense of being right as "Vanity". Even though Camus shares many of Meursault's feelings and ideas at the end of the novel (far more than he did at the start), Camus still maintains critical distance between himself as author and his protagonist. *The Stranger* is a novel not a philosophical manifesto.

The Temptation of Meursault

The purpose of the final chapter (and we may add here that it is the purpose of both Meursault as narrator and Camus as author) is to interpret all that has gone before and to come to an understanding of life on the basis of that interpretation. The structure is provided by a series of temptations which Meursault has to endure. This process of temptation forces upon him the self-analysis which he has avoided in the past, and it leads in turn to a heightened level of self-awareness. Faced with the imminence of his death by execution, Meursault can no longer ignore the reality of his mortality: there is a difference between contemplating the inevitability of death from the perspective of a healthy young man who might expect forty more years of life and contemplating certain execution within a matter of days: for the first time in his life, he reflects on the meaning of his own death *for him*.

Meursault has been moved to a cell from which "I see the sky, and that's all I see" (108). Under these circumstances, having neither routine to take up his time nor sense impressions to distract him, Meursault, a man who, by his own admission "pretty much lost the habit of analyzing [himself]," is forced by circumstances to consider the relationship between life and death as a philosopher might (65). In the process, a protagonist who has throughout the novel been clearly distinct from the author becomes a spokesperson at least for Camus' own understanding of man's relationship to the world in which he lives.

The first temptations are all based on denial of human mortality. It is entirely natural than a man condemned to death should feel that the prolongation of life (by twenty-four hours, by weeks or months, by years) is in itself desirable, that length of life is a value in and of itself, and that such a man should therefore spend his time hoping for some form of reprieve rather than confronting the imminence of his death. In this battle between Meursault's heart and his head (emotion versus reason), it is the latter which always brings him back to reality, exposing hope as an illusion no matter in what form it presents itself. When Meursault has purged himself of this form of hope, he is confronted by the transcendent temptation of belief in the after-life in the form of the chaplain's Christian faith. This process of temptation immediately prior to execution parallels the final temptation of Jesus Christ by Satan during Christ's forty days and forty nights in the Judean desert, an identification which (as we shall see) Camus makes quite explicit in the final lines of the novel.

When Meursault says, "All I care about right now is escaping the machinery of justice, seeing if there's any way out of the inevitable" (108), Camus uses the word "inevitable" to show the paradoxical nature of Meursault's endeavor. Meursault has forgotten the truth of the nurse's statement in Chapter 1 and of his own comment upon it, "'If you go slowly, you risk getting sunstroke. But if you go too fast, you work up a sweat and then catch a chill inside the church.' She was right. There was no way out" (17).

Length of Life Seen as a Value

The first half of this chapter chronicles the battle within Meursault; he uses all of his intellectual energy in a bid to negate the finality of his death sentence as though extending his life would somehow change the essential relationship between life and death. His first fantasy involves "escaping the relentless machinery" of justice (108). He laments never having studied accounts of prisoners going to the guillotine because he might have found one instance of someone who escaped. He knows that even a single instance would have given him "hope" and that, "My heart would have taken over from there" leading his "imagination" to construct scenarios where the condemned man makes a "leap to freedom … a wild run for it" (109). Fantasy, however, soon gives way to logic. Meursault is forced to acknowledge that a break for freedom would end with a "random bullet" in the back, and that even imagining such an end is a "luxury" since the "machinery" of justice would thus still take its inevitable course (109).

The Voice of Dissent

The first attempt to convince himself that he has a chance to extend his life having failed, Meursault turns to the diversion of mocking the disparity between the inevitability of the sentence being carried out and the comical, arbitrary way in which the sentence was arrived at. He comments that "there really was something ridiculously out of proportion between the verdict such certainty was based on and the imperturbable march of events from the moment the verdict was announced" (109). Meursault gives three reasons for finding the legal process which produced the verdict ludicrous: the sentence was read at 8 p.m. not 5 p.m., raising the possibility that a different verdict might have been given at a different time; the serious decision to kill a man was taken by men who that same day had taken the trivial decision of whether or not to change their underwear; and, finally, the verdict was given the authority of "some vague notion called the French … people" which Meursault finds to be a meaningless abstraction (109). Once again, however, Meursault is forced back to reality: despite the validity (in his own mind at least) of his criticisms, from the moment he was sentenced, the "consequences became as real and as serious as the wall against which I pressed the length of my body" (110).

Delaying the Inevitable

Next, Meursault returns to the "poisoned joy" of fantasy visualizing himself somehow freed from prison, attending executions as a spectator (as his father once had), and able to walk away after the event (110). Todd points out that Camus here draws on autobiography, "The story of Meursault's father attending an execution and then returning home and vomiting is a repetition of a story about his own father told to Camus by his grandmother and his mother. It was one of the few things that Camus knew about his father who was killed in the First World War before Camus reached the age of one year" (198). Meursault is reverting to the voyeuristic relationship which he had with life at the start of the novel, for example when he observed in a detached way the mourners at Maman's vigil or the local inhabitants enjoying their Sunday. In planning to go to "every execution ... to watch and then go and throw up afterwards," Meursault is envisaging himself as a spectator on human mortality, a stranger seeing the deaths of others whilst never himself dying (110). He soon realizes that it is "a mistake even to consider the possibility ... I wasn't being reasonable ... [I] let myself get carried away by such imaginings" (110). This time, however, when reality strikes down fantasy, Meursault pays a terrible price: his teeth chatter uncontrollably not from cold but from fear of death, and he rolls himself into the fetal position; hope is like a drug which gives a temporary high only at the cost of the prolonged agony of withdrawal.

The power of reason is merely temporary, and Meursault is soon fantasizing about reforming the entire legal system and devising a method of execution which gives the "condemned man" (who Meursault euphemistically terms "the patient") a chance of survival, "Even one in a thousand" (111). This leads him to speculate on the viability of a cocktail of chemicals which would kill in most but not quite all cases, thus giving "the patient" some basis for hope of survival which the guillotine denies, since "the trouble with the guillotine was that you had no chance at all, absolutely none" (111). This one chance (even "one in a thousand was good enough to set things right" [111]) would take away the despair of death because the "condemned man" could focus on the possibility of evading death; however, as the chaplain will later point out, all men are "condemned to die" and therefore no one can escape (117). It is, however, simple realism which ends these escapist imaginings. Meursault is "forced to admit" that the guillotine is a superior form of execution: not only does it never fail, but if "by some extraordinary chance" it should, then the process would just start over again (111). Meursault comes to recognize that the genius of the guillotine is that it forces the condemned man to hope that nothing goes wrong rather than to hope for some kind of malfunction; it forces the condemned man into what he calls "a kind of moral collaboration" willing that his own execution goes off without a hitch because any hitch will only add to the prisoner's fear without changing the outcome (111).

The Romantic Conception of Death

Having effectively dismissed all possibilities of escape at the last minute and of a malfunction in the machinery of justice, Meursault's next evasion is to cling to his romantically "exaggerated notions" that death by guillotine is somehow significant, dramatic and meaningful; that it offers a kind of immortality (112). This view, which is "something the imagination could hold on to," is based on Meursault's knowledge of the French Revolution: the condemned (a person of noble or event royal descent) climbs the steps up to a scaffold, makes a speech to the assembled multitude, and then is executed to accompanying drums and the shouts of the masses (112). If you are familiar with *A Tale of Two Cities*, think of Sydney Carton's final thoughts, "It is a far, far better thing that I do, than I have ever done; it is a far, far better rest that I go to than I have ever known." The memory of a newspaper article, however, forces Meursault to acknowledge that the reality is actually prosaic: the guillotine is a "simple … precision instrument" set up on the ground "on the same level as the man approaching it" which is "narrower" than Meursault imagined it, and it kills "discreetly, with a little shame and with great precision" (112). There is nothing at all for the imagination to hold on to: the victim is not remembered because death destroys "everything" (112).

Life-Extension

Despite the fact that his reason tells him "not to think of them anymore," there remain three further evasions to which Meursault clings: the dawn, his appeal, and the possibility of a last-minute pardon. Although he knows intellectually that death wipes out everything, Meursault still cannot bring himself to believe in the reality of his own death, "I would listen to my heartbeat. I couldn't imagine that this sound which had been with me for so long could ever stop" (112). The dawn is important to Meursault because he knows that, if he is not taken away by the time the sun comes up, he will have "gained another twenty-four hours" (112). He is clinging to life one day at a time because death terrifies him, but having gained more time he simply wastes it in fantasizing about his appeal which seems to offer the prospect not of extending life by hours but by months and perhaps by "20 more years of life" (112).

Meursault admits that this idea causes his heart to take a "terrifying leap" a phrase which encapsulates the paradox of Meursault's position: his fantasies offer the exciting leap of hope, but this leap is terrifying because intellectually he knows that the hope is based on illusion. Finally, reason wins out, and Meursault concludes that even the appeal would not change the essential dilemma of mortality, "Since we're going to die, it's obvious that when and how don't matter. Therefore … I had to accept the rejection of my appeal" (114). There is no appeal against mortality. Meursault draws the reader's attention to "all the reasoning which went into that 'therefore'" because it is vitally important that reason has triumphed over emotion (114). Meursault has constructed a syllogism: all men die; when death comes is irrelevant; therefore, the desire to extend the duration of life must be rejected.

There is one remaining distraction: the possibility of a complete pardon, the thought of which causes "the hot blood … [to] suddenly surge through my body and sting my eyes with a delirious joy" (114). Meursault has reached a point, however, when, by an act of will, he is able to control his self-destructive imagination and re-impose "level-headed" reason (115). He forces himself to argue logically that since he has rejected the idea of an appeal, he must also reject the idea of a pardon. Having done this, something remarkable happens: Meursault "gained an hour of calm" during which he is able to contemplate his imminent execution and yet still "feel the steady pulse of my blood circulating inside me" (115). He has finally overcome his fear of death. This means accepting a number of painful propositions: that Marie is now probably with another man, or sick, or even dead, and that, just as Marie no longer means anything to him, people will quickly forget him when he is dead. Meursault is rather surprised that not only is he able to contemplate these realities, but that it is not even hard to do it. Because of this new-found self-assurance, he is confident that, "I didn't need to see the chaplain" which makes it comically ironic that the chaplain chooses "that exact moment" to intrude upon Meursault – a classic example of being just the wrong person, in the wrong place, at the wrong time (115).

Showalter correctly argues that, for the novel to succeed, "Somewhere in Meursault's final illumination, Camus must give us insight into the fallacy in his attitude that led him so thoughtlessly to take another person's life" (96). The chaplain is the catalyst which produces this insight.

The Confrontation with the Chaplain:

The intrusion of the chaplain, directly against Meursault's wishes, represents the final attempt of a coercive society to make him conform. Ironically, the interview has precisely the opposite effect, for Meursault's confrontation with the chaplain leads to a final epiphany ("a sudden, intuitive perception of or insight into the reality or essential meaning of something, usually initiated by some simple, homely, or commonplace occurrence or experience" [Dictionary.com]). Doubrovsky defines the essential nature of Meursault's epiphany thus, "the imminence of death makes explicit those values which heretofore have been implicit only" (75). A careful reading of these closing pages of the novel is essential to understanding the life-changing insight which Meursault achieves.

Meursault's initial reaction to the appearance of the chaplain is a "little shudder" since his untimely appearance suggests that he has come to bring news of the rejection of Meursault's appeal and of the imminence of his execution (115). There is no return, however, to the terror which Meursault experiences in the days after his conviction. In fact, Meursault calmly explains to the chaplain the distinction between "extreme despair" on the one hand and being "afraid" on the other (116). Whilst Meursault willingly acknowledges that he fears execution, "which was only natural," he insists that he does not feel "desperate" in the face of death (116). It is on this basis that he explains to the chaplain that he has no interest in Christianity though he is perfectly willing to acknowledge the "right" of others to seek consolation in its beliefs (117).

Unable to accept this rejection of his theology, the chaplain continues to try to persuade Meursault to turn to God. Interestingly, both the chaplain and Meursault begin from exactly the same assumption: the chaplain argues that all men are "condemned to die" and then says, "'if you don't die today, you'll die tomorrow, or the next day'" (117) which exactly parallels the understanding which Meursault reached only hours or days earlier, "Since we're all going to die, it's obvious that when and how don't matter" (114). The difference between their viewpoints is clearly defined in the following exchange, "'Have you no hope at all? And do you really live with the thought that when you die, you die, and nothing remains?' 'Yes,' I said" (117). This calm, monosyllabic response, the self-confident language of dissent, shows how different Meursault is now from the man who attempted to avoided a discussion of religious belief with the magistrate by appearing to accept the magistrate's position commenting on his evasion that "whenever I want to get rid of someone I'm not really listening to, I made it appear as if I agree with them" (69). Meursault is bored by the chaplain because, unlike the chaplain, he no longer finds the idea of the finality of death to be a "[t]errifying ordeal … more than a man could bear" (117). Meursault's struggle with the temptation of hope has purged him of the need for consolation, and he is able to tell the chaplain that he will go to his death calmly without despair.

Religious Consolation in the Face of Man's Mortality

The religious view of the relationship between life and death is summarized in Hamlet's statement, "If it be now, / 'tis not to come; if it be not to come, it will be / now; if it be not now, yet it will come. The / readiness is all" (*Hamlet* 5.2). At this point in the play, Hamlet has rediscovered his faith in God and is prepared to accept death whenever it comes: the sole purpose of this life is to purify the soul so that whenever death comes one's soul is ready to enter the superior after-life for eternity. The problem which Meursault has with this view of the relationship between life and death is expressed in Camus' statement, "If there is sin against life, it consists not so much in despairing of life as in hoping for another life and in eluding the implacable grandeur of this life" (*Myth* 153).

Despairing of life is at least honest: it is Meursault's condition in Part One of the novel when, almost despite himself, he does experience some of life's pleasures, albeit in a debased form. However, to concentrate exclusively on the after-life is to ignore entirely the pleasures of life like some ascetic monk locked away from the distractions of the material world to contemplate the attainment of spiritual purity.

McCarthy points out the irony that the intervention of the chaplain, his attempt to impose transcendental values, causes Meursault to "assert the kind of life he had lived in Part 1, and of which he became gradually aware in Part 2" which is why, when asked to look into the stone walls of his prison for the fact of God, he says that he only ever found there the face of his lover Marie (69). This explains what Meursault means when he says of the chaplain, "He wasn't even sure he was alive, because he was living like a dead man" (120). The paradox which strikes Meursault here is that even though he is going to face death within days, whilst the chaplain has many years to live, Meursault is the only one of the two who is actually living the life which remains to him.

The Voice of Dissent in the Final Epiphany

In his 1943 review of the novel, Maurice Blanchot draws attention to "a rather awkward change in tone between the almost absolute objectivity of the narration that is its profound truth and the last pages, where the stranger expresses what he thinks and what he feels in the face of death and life" (quoted in Gay-Crosier 105). What Blanchot is describing (quite accurately) is the moment in the novel when Meursault, who in the courtroom could give no coherent account of his life, literally finds his voice, and it is the voice of dissent. Camus explained the change in Meursault in this way, "With the chaplain, my Stranger doesn't justify himself. He becomes angry; that's quite different. So you say that it's I who's doing the explaining here then? Yes, and I thought about that a great deal. I decided on it because I wanted my character to come to the only great problem by means of the daily and the natural" (Carnets quoted in Brosman 140).

Meursault realizes that the chaplain's certainties are illusions which allow the man to evade the what is for him the terrifying truth about life; in contrast, Meursault is "sure of my life and sure of the death I had waiting for me" (120). This is symbolized by Meursault's rejection of the chaplain's final temptation that he perceive in the stones of his prison "a divine face emerge from … [your] darkness" (119). Meursault replies that he has never sought God's face in the stones but only the face of Marie and that even that was in vain. He now accepts the stones for what they are, as he accepts the whole physical world for what it is, without imposing transcendent values upon it.

The chaplain's "certainties" are not worth a single hair on a woman's head because the latter is real and the former merely abstract fantasies designed to avoid having to face reality. The chaplain is, in fact, terrified of death, but Meursault is not because he is now completely accepting of the fact that the indeterminate period between birth and death is "all I had" (201); it is now all he *needs*. This is why he says with a triumphant tone, "I had been right, I was still right, I was always right. I had lived my life one way and I could just as well have lived it another … It was as if I had waited all this time … to be vindicated" (121). This is not the sweeping vindication of everything Meursault thought and did in Part One which it is often taken to be – far from it. It is an unambiguous assertion of man's freedom to act.

The reader recalls all of those times in Part One when Meursault doubted that he was right, felt that he had done or said something wrong, apologized out of guilt, pretended to agree with someone just to prevent further discussion, or felt that others were judging him. Now the doubts have been replaced by conviction: at every moment in one's life one can either shoot or not shoot because one is completely free. Nothing matters because when you die that wipes out everything – something which, under his fragile faith, the chaplain knows very well. The chaplain is a hypocrite because he is teaching a form of consolation in which he does not himself believe. This is made clear by a self-revelatory statement when the chaplain tells Meursault "almost as if it wasn't me he was talking to … [that] sometimes we think we're sure when in fact we're not" (116). The man does not believe in the redemption into eternal life which he offers Meursault as a protection from despair: the chaplain is here unconsciously speaking of the fragility of his own faith, a fragility which is contrasted with Meursault's certainty.

Meursault as narrator now writes from the perspective of full understanding. He is very far from approving of the way he once lived his life. He points very clearly to a fatal flaw in his earlier understanding of the relationship between life and death, "Throughout the whole absurd life I'd lived, a dark wind had been rising towards me from somewhere deep in my future, across years that were still to come, and as it passed, this wind leveled was offered to me at the time" (121). Knowing that death was the end, Meursault here describes the way in which this truth formerly crippled him because the fear of the future that it engendered made it impossible for him to appreciate the happiness of life in the moment. Having overcome that fear, Meursault finally comes to understand that "we're all elected by the same fate, me and billions and billions of privileged people … Everybody was privileged. There were only privileged people" (121). The privilege is that each of us has the time between birth and death: we have done nothing to deserve it; no God has given it; it does not mean anything; everything will be erased at death; and yet within that brief period happiness is possible. To *know this*, is to be privileged, to be a person. We are all "brothers" in that we are all "condemned," but humanity is divided into those who face that truth rationally and those who irrationally deny it, those who embrace the privilege of life and those who reject it.

The revelation which causes Meursault to feel "that I had been happy, and that I was happy again" comes as a surprise to him and marks the moment when Meursault moves from instinctive to conscious understanding of the absurd (123). In doing so, he has become for the first time in the novel an Absurdist – one who, "Assured of his temporally limited freedom, of his revolt devoid of future, and of his moral consciousness ... lives out his adventure within the span of his lifetime" (*Myth* 66). That this understanding has implications for morality is clear from Camus' own admission in a letter written to Claude de Fréminville on December 12th, 1940, "I've done a lot of foolish things for some time, and foolish things do not result in happiness either for others or for myself" (quoted in Todd 119). Once one acknowledges that happiness is a value and that certain actions can result in happiness for oneself, then one must logically add that one's actions necessarily also have implications for the happiness of others, as Camus does in the above quotation.

Authentic Existence

Exhausted but calm following his rejection of everything for which the chaplain stands, Meursault, for the first time in the novel, consciously experiences the true beauty of the natural world, "I woke up with the stars in my face. Sounds of the countryside were drifting in. Smells of night, earth and salt air were cooling my temples. The wondrous peace of that sleeping summer flowed through me like a tide" (122). It is significant here that Meursault experiences the world with all five of his senses simultaneously. He is fully involved in the experience. In fact, he feels himself to be part of the world, neither its beneficiary nor its victim, but one with the stars, the earth and the air. This is very different from the romantic illusion of being in harmony with the world. Meursault understands that the world "forever meant nothing to me" in exactly the same way as he means nothing to the world (122). Thus, the second essential element of Meursault's epiphany is that he comes to understand that our lives are lived out in a world which is neither malevolent nor benevolent, "I opened myself to the gentle indifference of the world. Finding it so much like myself – so like a brother really" (122-3). This corrects a fundamental error in Meursault's earlier thinking.

One could argue that he has always unconsciously felt this but has never been able to believe it. Part One of the novel describes Meursault as at times feeling that the sun is benevolent ("I was absorbed by the feeling that the sun was doing me a lot of good" [50]) and at other times that it is malevolent ("the day, already bright with sun, hit me like a slap in the fact" [47]). This is an error which results from Meursault's hypersensitivity to sensual impressions: unable, in the days of his value-free freedom, to make meaningful choices, he was as much the victim of his physical environment as he was of his social environment which, as we have seen, led directly to the shooting of the Arab. The epiphany fundamentally changes his view of how to live his life: only the man who doubts his freedom needs to shoot because he feels the need to assert that freedom; the man who knows that he lives his life in complete freedom does not need to shoot. To put it simply: life is meaningless, but this is not the same as saying that life is without value to the individual, and once one recognizes that one's own life can have value, once must recognize that this is true of all men.

Meursault's Relationship with his Mother

A final effect of Meursault's epiphany is that, again for the first time in the novel, he comes to understand, and even to empathize with, his mother in her final years. When the director of the old people's home describes her relationship with her "fiancé" Perez, he clearly presents it as a whimsical, somewhat humorous aberration of two elderly people, a view shared by the other old people who used to "'tease'" Perez (12). In contrast, Meursault now takes his mother's affair very seriously, "I felt as if I understood why at the end of her life she had taken a 'fiancé' … So close to death, Maman must have felt free then and ready to live it all again … and I felt ready to live it all again … that blind rage had washed me clean, rid me of hope" (122). What Meursault has understood (it is the central message of the novel) is that we cannot truly live until we have accepted both that life has no meaning and that death is nothing to fear; man is alone and none of his actions has any impact on an indifferent world. This, Meursault realizes, is the state of freedom which his mother reached in her final years when she could no longer evade the reality of her fast-approaching death. Meursault identifies this as the same state that he has now reached, "Maman must have felt free then and ready to live it all again" (122). The freedom which his mother gains when she finally faces with calm acceptance the prospect of her own death is a kind of re-birth; it is as though she has finally understood how life should be lived, and she takes a fiancé because it makes her happy so to do.

Meursault understands that it was a delightful game in which she "played at beginning again" (122). This is what makes Maman different from the chaplain (and indeed from every other character in the book): Maman is conscious of her self-delusion and is not therefore deluded at all. Interestingly, Meursault's belated understanding and appreciation of his mother appears to mirror Camus' changing attitude to his own mother. Lottman comments that the "silent, submissive figure … [of Catherine Camus] became a more marvelous woman to her son as he grew older. In his earlier books … he seemed to blame his mother for his condition as *étranger*. Now [in his unfinished novel *The First Man*] she is seen to have been the *étrangere*" (25).

Meursault's understanding of his mother also explains the previously inexplicable fact that, "'[Maman] expressed to her friends her desire for a religious burial'" (6). When told this by the director, Meursault is simply confused since, "While not an atheist, Maman had never in her life given a thought to religion" (6). Now, Meursault completely understands his mother's action and, though he remains an atheist himself, has total acceptance of it. There is actually no mystery at all: Maman chose a religious burial because she chose a religious burial; that is, she made a free choice because that choice made her happy.

In Maman's case (and this is where she is completely unlike either the magistrate or the chaplain on the one hand or the Meursault who undergoes temptation in prison on the other), it is a completely free choice, not a choice motivated by some desperate hope of life beyond the grave or even of extending her life on earth by a few more years. This is why Meursault (who is basically put on trial for not weeping at his mother's death) asserts that, "Nobody, nobody had the *right* to cry over her" (emphasis added 122). Much is made by the prosecution at his trial of the fact that Perez does not see Meursault cry. We are supposed to cry at funerals; social convention dictates that we ought not only be sad but show that we are sad. Meursault, however, now asserts the very opposite: in crying for a person's death, we are infringing his/her individuality by imposing our own values upon another human being. Maman is privileged to live her life the way she chooses to live it, and we have no right to assume that she fears or regrets her death just because we fear and regret our own death.

Meursault as Christ-Figure

Just as his mother chooses her form of burial, Meursault now chooses the form of his death. He feels that "for everything to be consummated" it is necessary to have "a large crowd of spectators ... [to] greet me with cries of hate" (123). Camus' protagonist dies a defiant rebel. The crowd would be composed of every other character in the novel, and Meursault feels that they should hate him because he has exposed their existence as an absurd farce which evades the truth about human life and human death. During his second interrogation by the magistrate, the man asks Meursault, "'Do you want my life to be meaningless?'" (69). The crowd will hate Meursault because his certainty does make their lives meaningless. Michael Delahoyde sums up the significance of this moment thus, "By suffering final judgment from the world, he realizes that he is no longer bound to conform to their standards ... the 'cries of hate' would be proof that he did not exist in the world's acceptance, but rather in a world of his own creation." This final wish also illustrates how far Meursault has developed from the accused on trial who was almost driven to tears by the hatred he perceived directed towards him: he has truly achieved indifference.

Meursault uses the word "consummated." Camus selects this word to recall to the reader's mind the statement made by Jesus on the cross: immediately after receiving the wine from the sponge at the end of the soldier's spear, John records, "When Jesus had tasted it, he said, 'It is finished!' Then he bowed his head and released his spirit" (John 19:30 *New Living Translation* 2007). However, in the Latin Vulgate this is recorded as "consumatum est," and Jesus' words are often translated, "It is consummated" (*The Douay-Rheims Bible*). Either way, the statement indicates that Jesus has finished what he came into the world to accomplish which is to redeem man from his sins by his crucifixion. By comparing Meursault with Jesus, Camus draws attention to the significance of the truth to which Meursault has just testified and for which he will be executed: it is a truth which redeems us from the poisonous joy of transcendent meaning. Just as Jesus destroyed the world of pagan worship and swept away its comforting certainties with his paradoxical truth, so now does Meursault destroy the Christian myth and sweep away its "certainties" (120). Camus' use of religious diction at the conclusion of the novel echoes a statement from his Notebooks, "'I am happy on this earth ... for my kingdom is of this earth" (quoted in Brée *Albert Camus* 13) which is a deliberate inversion of Jesus' statement, "My kingdom is not of this world" (John 18:36). Brée instructively quotes Camus as writing (in a preface the novel twelve years after its initial publication), "'in the person of my character [Meursault] I tried to create the only Christ we deserve'" (quoted in *Albert Camus* 20).

Summary:

Although they do not admit it, most people find the idea of a death in which "nothing remains" to be a "terrifying ordeal" causing "extreme despair ... more than a man can bear" (117).

At the start of this chapter, Meursault also feels this terror of death.

Meursault eventually sees that extending one's life-span does not change the fact of mortality.

Meursault realizes that all men have "only a little time left" (120) and that we should not waste it on things which do not interest us.

Meursault realizes that he was right to believe that we are all free to live the life we choose.

Meursault realizes that he has mistaken the nature of man's relationship with the world, and now feels that the pursuit of individual happiness gives life value.

Understanding what he now understands, Meursault would not have shot the Arab.

Afterword

> I have too much taste for life and a feeling for the world to believe that all is nothingness … I do not believe that negation encompasses everything, I only believe that it is the beginning of everything. (Camus, letter to Jacques de Vriendt, 1945, quoted in Todd 215)

Despite, or perhaps because of, its apparent simplicity, *The Stranger* has frequently been misunderstood. The fundamental source of the misunderstanding is a failure to distinguish between the protagonist and the author, particularly at the end of the novel. In the absence of a third person omniscient narrator, each reader is left to decide to what degree the author's views coincide with those which Meursault expresses in the last hours of his life. In answering this vital question, it is important to keep in mind the injunction of British novelist D. H. Lawrence, "Never trust the teller, trust the tale."

In his re-assessment of the novel "after forty years," Harold Bloom's impression is of "evasive hedonism, uncertain of its own gestures," and he concludes that Meursault "seems even smaller now than he did four decades ago when his dry disengagement had a certain novelty" (Bloom 401). Bloom critically examines René Girard's argument that Camus is guilty of "'literary solipsism'" in *The Stranger* because Meursault, who has murdered another human being, is presented by Camus as being immune from the judgment which Meursault himself makes of other characters. However, Bloom's defense of the novel against this criticism, and his assertion that the novel is neither "morally flawed or inconsistent," rests on his dismissive view that the action of the novel takes place in a cosmos in which "guilt and innocence are indistinguishable, and Jewish or Christian judgments are hopelessly irrelevant": Meursault (who is interested in neither events nor in himself) is simply "an inadequate consciousness dazed by the sun, overwhelmed by a context that is too strong for him" (Bloom 402).

The problem with Bloom's interpretation is that it takes Meursault's conviction that the sun (and the world which it represents) is malevolent as being somehow endorsed by Camus. In fact, Meursault only sees the sun in this way at certain times in the novel (one of them certainly being at the time he murders the Arab); at other times (for example, lying on the beach with Marie), he makes the equally erroneous judgment that the sun is benevolent. Bloom is wrong to assert that the idea of a malevolent sun contradicts the conception of an indifferent world because the Meursault who finally comes to understand the truth about his relationship with the world is neither intellectually nor morally the same person who shot the Arab, an essential point which Camus makes perfectly clear.

The central importance of the progression in the consciousness of the protagonist is illustrated by Camus' initial outline of the novel which became *The Stranger*. Olivier Todd records that, in the autumn of 1937, Camus wrote that the novel would be about, "A man who looked for life where it is normally found, in marriage and a job, etc., notices all at once after reading a fashion catalogue, how he had been a stranger [étranger] to his own life, life as it is portrayed in fashion catalogues" (65). Obviously, much changed in the writing of the novel, most notably that Meursault's epiphany results from his confrontation with the chaplain rather than with a fashion magazine. However, the essential element of sudden revelation remains. In the original plan, the revelation was to be the understanding by Meursault that he has lived his absurd life in an inauthentic way; in the novel as it finally evolved, the revelation is both more complex and more satisfying. Meursault realizes that his instinctive understanding of the absurdity of life was correct, but that from that understanding he drew erroneous conclusions about how to live the absurd life. Brée supports this view when she argues that the significance in what Lawrence would call the tale of Meursault's killing of the Arab "seems to lie in the revelation of the basic and dangerous inadequacy ... [of the] 'indifferent Man'" (*Albert Camus* 20).

A more helpful way of interpreting the novel than that of Bloom is provided by Robert Champigny who argues that in Part Two of *The Stranger* "the ethos of Meursault is confronted with pseudo-ethics. From a philosophical standpoint, that is what the trial consists of" (124). Champigny defines pseudo-ethics as the "attempt to give meaning, values to a life by viewing it as part of a whole" when in reality there is no whole, no totality (124), and he concludes that Meursault is a threat to society precisely because he shatters the concept of the whole giving value to the one, "The global effect of Meursault's retort to the priest is a rejection of pseudo-values and the affirmation of existential values" (125). This gives us a context in which to fully understand the significance of Meursault's assertion, "I had been right, I was still right, I was always right. I had lived my life one way and I could just as well have lived it another" (121). The protagonist is asserting that values exist *because* he has come to understand that not all views of human existence are equally valid. The difference between Meursault and the forces that find him to be a monster who must be destroyed, Champigny explains, is that Meursault "considers his life as one life-unit among others," generating his values from his own experience of life and rejecting the right of society to impose its pseudo-values upon his individual life (125).

Up until his final epiphany, Meursault narrates the events of his life chronologically without connecting them into a coherent narrative; he concentrates solely on the moment in which he finds himself, without reference to past occurrences or future consequences. That is what is changed by the realization that he "had been happy and … was happy again" (123). As Lewis writes, "It is Meursault's destiny, like that of many another tragic hero, to suffer toward the discovery of his own identity, to take upon himself, knowingly at the last, the burden of humanity" (quoted in Bloom ed. 55). There is nothing evasive or uncertain about the way Meursault does this.

At a point where he can no longer regard death as merely a theoretical possibility in some ill-defined future, Meursault has learned that "life with all its inexplicable involvements is not only worth living, but that it offers man his one chance of happiness ... [Life] is in reality an invitation to happiness completely rooted in the knowledge that men live and men die" (Rhein 35). Because of death, nothing matters, but once one has faced this reality without fear one comes to the understanding that because of death, nothing matters *except being alive*. Most people miss this truth through their denial of death: they are living for the after-life. The value, the significance of life, the meaning which each individual can choose to give to life is only evident in the face of death.

McCarthy correctly interprets what it is that Meursault finally comes to understand, but he fails to see how it relates to the narrative as a whole. Whilst conceding that Meursault finally comes to understand the nature of human existence, McCarthy argues that this explanation does not allow "the reader retrospectively to interpret Part 1... The two parts do not fit neatly together, and the more disturbing features of Part 1 must be forgotten before the reader's sympathy and understanding may be won" (McCarthy 29). McCarthy presumably has in mind Meursault's writing of the letter to the Arab girl, his refusal to intervene when he hears Raymond beating her, and, most significantly, the shooting of the Arab, for none of which does Meursault ever express regret or remorse. The novel is found to be incoherent, in effect, because Meursault does not apply to his own conduct the same values which he readily applies to the conduct of others.

Essentially, the objection is that Camus does not provide an explanation, a moral homily at the end of the story, which is perhaps what Sartre had in mind when he termed *The Stranger* a novel "that does not explain" (Sartre quoted in McCarthy 27). However, just because the narrator does not explain does not mean that there is no explanation in the tale which the narrator tells: put simply, Camus refuses to do the reader's work. Meursault's estrangement from the values on which society rests is ultimately a dead end which in Part One leads him not only to fail to see any connection between his actions (such as the writing of a letter and the brutalization of a young woman) but to killing another person. Life is absurd, but that does not justify Meursault's complete abdication of personal responsibility, and this is what he finally realizes. It is vital for the reader to remember here that the first word of Meursault's narrative is written/spoken/thought *after* the action of the narrative has been completed. Brée explains the importance of this when she argues that Meursault comes to understand both why he "acquiesced to the 'natural death' of his mother" and why he "participated in the death of another human being" and that this understanding "goes deeper than guilt and remorse" (*Albert Camus* 19). She goes on to offer the following explication (which I regard as the most brilliant one hundred and thirty-five words ever written on this novel):

> The awakening that follows his death sentence alone can bring into focus those two moments unifying the pattern of his existence. Meursault sees, at last, that to exist is happiness. His indifference to the sights and smells of the world turns into a conscious love; his passive acquiescence to the violence done human beings turns into a passionate revolt against death and a sense of human fraternity. He can now understand the small joys that filled the last days of his mother's humble life. The revolver shot that precipitated him from his semi-conscious existence into the closed world of his mind has, as its counterpart, the violent act of consciousness whereby Meursault emerges from his isolation assuming his identity as a human being, the full responsibility for his life in its beauty and incomprehensible strangeness. (*Albert Camus* 19).

Paradoxically, although death means that all actions are possible, that all are equal, that nothing matters, that at any moment one may shoot or not shoot, the reality of human happiness means that all actions are not equal, cannot ever be equal. Once Meursault realizes that he "had been happy and …

was happy again," he could not have chosen to shoot the Arab precisely *because he knows* that he is free to shoot the Arab (123).

In my experience of teaching this novel, students have mixed feeling about the ending. Some find the insight which Meursault gains to be entirely satisfying, even life-changing, while others feel that the resolution still leaves the important questions unanswered. For the former, the privilege of knowing that we mortals freely live in an indifferent world is enough. The latter, however, feel that this truth is only a starting point and that it begs the question of *how* individuals and groups *should* live in a world without transcendental values; essentially they criticize the novel on the grounds that it confronts, but offers no solution to, "the eternal problem of the basis of morality if one does not believe in God" (Todd 156). Ironically, Camus expressed a similar reservation when he wrote in his review of Sartre's *La Nausée*, "To observe that life is absurd is not an end, but a beginning" (quoted in Todd 84). Harold Bloom makes the same point when he writes, "Meursault is not as yet an impressive person as the book closes, but he has begun to change, to feel, to choose, to will" (emphasis in original Bloom ed. 9). In this statement, if not in others, Bloom perfectly captures the author's intention in *The Stranger*. Breé and Lynes Jr. in their introduction to the first American textbook edition of *The Stranger* go much further. They describe Meursault's epiphany as "a kind of spiritual awakening" and conclude of Meursault that "[i]f life were granted him he could begin to construct a new system of values and perhaps discover vital links between himself and other men" (quoted in Showalter 14). The remainder of Camus' literary output (and, indeed, of his personal life) would be an attempt to explore what this beginning leads to.

Camus himself came to feel that *The Stranger* placed too much emphasis on the individual and that a "different order of understanding and ethics was necessary, one that encompassed others rather than isolating the individual subject. Society, not the individual, was now the measure of meaning" (Zaretsky

58). Writing in 1955 to the critic Roland Barthes, Camus made a distinction between *The Stranger*, which he said represented *révolte solitaire*, and *The Plague* which he saw as a transition to the recognition of community (Lottman 543). Indeed, he would eventually write in his *Carnets*, "I see clearly that absurd thought ... ends in an impasse, and the problem is, Can one live in an impasse?" (quoted in Todd 167). This explains Camus' own involvement as an engaged artist in the political and social questions of his day.

Appendix 1: *A Happy Death* (1936-1938, unpublished in Camus' lifetime)

> For if there is a sin against life, it consists perhaps not so much in despairing of life as in hoping for another life and in eluding the implacable grandeur of this life … for, contrary to the general belief, hope equals resignation. And to live is not to resign oneself. (Camus "Summer in Algiers" in *Myth* 153)

In *A Happy Death*, Camus' first novel, the protagonist, Patrice Mersault, shares more than a surname with the Meursault of *The Stranger*: each is a shipping clerk working in Algiers, and each kills a man. An early Camus manuscripts bears as a subtitle "L'Etranger ou Un home heureux." Catherine Brosman comments that this wording, combining as it does the titles of the two later novels *La Mort heureuse* and *L'Etranger*, "show[s] not only the connection between the novels, which is integral, but also their common source in an earlier conception" (43). Many of the ideas explored in *The Stranger* are also evident in *A Happy Death*; indeed, the general consensus of critical opinion is that the earlier work was abandoned because Camus found in *The Stranger* a way of bringing together characters, settings, events and themes which remain disjointed and incoherent in *A Happy Death*.

The chronology (though not the literary structure) of both novels is essentially the same: the protagonist lives an inauthentic life in Algiers; he commits a murder; he thereby attains the potential for living (and dying) authentically. Patrice's life in Algiers is dominated by the eight hours of every day which he spends at the office and the sensual pleasure he pursues in his leisure. He is much more aware than is Mersault that the time he spends working takes away his freedom which indicates that from the start of the novel Patrice is much more consciously in "revolt" than is Mersault (*Happy* 41). In conversation with Patrice, the cripple Zagreus makes the point that "it takes time to be happy," and that it takes money to buy that time (*Happy* 43). The solution to Patrice's problem is to shoot Zagreus and take the considerable fortune which the crippled man had accumulated before the accident which left him paralyzed. Patrice is now free to pursue single-mindedly the happiness he has wanted all of his life.

The shooting of the crippled man raises the same moral problems as the shooting of the Arab; indeed, in his excellent Afterward, Jean Sarocchi refers to Patrice as taking advantage of Zagreus' trust in him to commit cold-blooded murder. This, however, ignores the fact that Zagreus is at the very least a willing co-conspirator in his own murder providing Patrice with the motive, the means and the opportunity. Zagreus wants Patrice to have the money to pursue what he calls Patrice's "'duty … to live and be happy'" (*Happy* 38).

Although he now has the time to achieve a happy life, Patrice fails. He travels throughout Europe, returns to Algiers and lives for some time with three girls at the (aptly named) House Above the World, marries Lucienne, lives in isolation at a house in the Chenoua which overlooks the sea. (The exact relationship of these events is somewhat unclear.) It is only when he becomes terminally ill with heart failure brought on by pleurisy (ironically first evident a few hours after he kills Zagreus) that Patrice feels "he had at last attained what he was seeking … [he] realized that his life and his fate were completed here and that henceforward all his efforts would be to submit to this happiness and to confront its terrible truth" (*Happy* 139-140). He understands that Lucienne will love another man once he is dead; he understands that authenticity of being cannot be measured in years; he has achieved the state of happiness. He dies with a smile because he does not fear death.

Appendix 2: *The Myth of Sisyphus* (first published 1942)

What follows makes no pretense to be anything more than a summary (and, quite frankly, a simplification) of Camus' essay. I have resisted the temptation to make direct connections with *The Stranger* leaving that to the reader who will find much to connect.

In his essay *The Myth of Sisyphus*, Camus addresses what he terms "the fundamental question of philosophy" and in doing so makes a crucial distinction between existentialism and absurdism (*Myth* 3). Put simply, since life clearly has no meaning, can there be any moral objection to suicide? Not to leave the reader in any doubt, Camus states his conclusion in the Preface: "even if one does not believe in God, suicide is not legitimate" (*Myth* v). Indeed, Camus calls his essay "a lucid invitation to live and to create, in the very midst of the desert [of nihilism]" (*Myth* v).

Camus argues that most people live their lives out of "habit," but that once confronted with the truth of "a world suddenly divested of illusions and lights, a man feels an alien, a stranger" who understands that the habits by which he and his fellows live are "ridiculous" (*Myth* 6). The absurd is defined as an individual's awareness of the mismatch between the assumptions upon which he has been living his life and the reality of that life. Thus, the absurd rests neither in the world not in man but rather in the confrontation between the "unreasonable silence of the world" and man's "wild longing for clarity" and meaning (*Myth* 28, 21). Once a man has confronted the truth that "reason is useless and there is nothing beyond reason," he lives in continual surprise that "everyone lives as if no one 'knew'" (*Myth* 35, 15). It is this which sets the stranger apart from society, for he alone is living in a world of "anguish" from which there is no escape because once a man recognizes absurdity it becomes "a passion, the most harrowing of all" (*Myth* 24, 22). The world no longer has anything to offer such a man except boredom when he "strives to quash it [anguish] in him and benumb it; terror when the mind contemplates death" (*Myth* 24).

Next, Camus reviews the thoughts of a number of existential philosophers (Heidegger, Jaspers, Shestov, Kierkegaard, and Husserl) on this essential human dilemma and concludes that "all of them without exception suggest escape" by making negation their new God, an external value which they reach not by reason but by a leap of faith taken at the point at which reason ends, and to this extent, Camus argues that these philosophers represent a dead end which he terms "philosophical suicide" (*Myth* 32, 41). In a footnote one page 42, Camus makes it clear that his objection is not to "the affirmation of God" but to the use of logic to get the thinker to a point where that affirmation seems to make life meaningful. The essential problem, for Camus, is not to blind oneself to the absurd but to take the absurd as a starting point and then to consider whether life is possible "in the face of the cruel mathematics that command our condition" (*Myth* 16). Camus accepts the absurd "contradiction between man's desire for clarity and unity and the world's irrationality, disunity, and fragmentation" (Rhein 28).

The solution which Camus proposes he terms "revolt" which he defines as "the certainty of a crushing fate, without the resignation that ought to accompany it" (*Myth* 54). The absurd man is determined to live on the basis only of what reason tells him, and reason tells him that he is unable to perceive meaning in life. Whilst suicide ends the confrontation with the absurd, "the man condemned to death" does the opposite by living defiantly in the face of "his only truth" (*Myth* 55). Most people live with the illusion of freedom because, imagining a purpose to life, they adapt their actions to furthering that purpose this relinquishing the very freedom which they see themselves as enjoying. In contrast, the absurd man lives with true freedom of action choosing to contemplate (like a condemned man at dawn) "the pure flame of life" which exists in a "world in which nothing is possible but everything is given, and beyond which all is collapse and nothingness" (*Myth* 60). Here is the paradox on which Camus' position rests: the meaninglessness of life is an "invitation to death," but by "the mere activity of consciousness I transform [it] into a rule of life," and in doing so I live life to the "maximum" because I live in true freedom (*Myth* 64, 63). The absurd man lives life passionately because each moment assumes the precious quality of the final moment of life – which, of course, each moment might be. Such a life is not, and can never be, personally meaningless.

To summarize, the absurd man lives without appeal to eternal values. Like an actor, he travels a "dead-end path"; the only difference is that for the actor the end comes after three hours and for the absurd man it comes after a lifetime (*Myth* 80).Within this lifetime, he knows that everything is permitted since morality derives from eternal values. However, Camus insists that the absurd "does not authorize all actions … [It] merely confers an equivalence on the consequences of these actions" which is not at all the same as saying that "nothing is forbidden" (*Myth* 67).

Camus provides sketches of the absurd man as lover (Don Juan), actor and conqueror to illustrate that life is possible based on the belief that "man is his own end … he is his only end … [and that if] he aims to be something, it is in this life" (*Myth* 67). Indeed, Camus concludes that the absurd, meaningless, Godless world is actually populated by individuals (a tiny fraction of the total population to be sure) "who think clearly and have ceased to hope" (*Myth* 92).

Finally, having established that it is possible to live by following "the commandments of the absurd," Camus turns to the questions of whether it is possible to create art (and particularly novels) from the same perspective (*Myth* 102). To do so, the novelist faces an inevitable conflict: the novel inherently requires its own "logic … reasonings … intuition … postulates … [and] clarity" all of which are alien to the absurd man who, knowing that he can neither explain nor solve, must be content with "experiencing and describing … [knowing that] Everything begins with lucid indifference" (*Myth* 100, 94). Camus gives a detailed interpretation of the works of Dostoevsky and Kafka concluding that both authors ultimately belong to existentialism rather than absurdism because each finds ground for hope. In the case of Dostoevsky, Camus points to the last pages of his final novel which contain Aliocha's assertion of faith in an eternal afterlife as proving that the author's world continues "to cherish its blind hopes," and in the case of Kafka, Camus points to K's break with Frieda and his move towards the Barnabas sisters as a leap of faith to God which Camus finds similar to the thinking of Kierkegaard (*Myth* 111, 133). Thus, both authors are rejected because, in the final analysis, hope is seen still to exist whilst "the [truly] tragic work might be the work that, after all future hope is exiled, describes the life of a happy man, and against this criterion Nietzsche appears to be the only artist to have derived the extreme consequences of the aesthetic of the Absurd" (*Myth* 137).

Sisyphus is presented as a true absurd hero not because he is condemned to push a rock up a hill and watch it roll back down again for all eternity but because he pushes the rock knowing that he will be pushing it for all eternity. He is made tragic precisely by his consciousness of the hopelessness of his case, and since he is thinking lucidly and without illusion, he is happy because the absurd and happiness are the "inseparable," being "two sons of the same earth" (*Myth* 122). The absurd man turns away from hope (and the subterfuges invented by generations of men to perpetuate hope) to concentrate on life itself; he becomes free. He then finds that the "struggle towards the heights is enough to fill a man's heart" (*Myth* 123).

Put very simply, Sisyphus' fate is tragic (he rolls the rock up the mountain only for all of his effort to be entirely wiped out when it inevitably rolls back down the mountain), unless, fully aware of what will happen, Sisyphus takes happiness from the very act of rolling the stone.

Appendix 3: "An Explication of *The Stranger*" by Jean-Paul Sartre

Sartre's essay on Camus' novel appeared in the February 1943 issue of the magazine *Cahiers du Sud*. The two would not meet until June 1st. However, Camus read the article, and Lottman reports that he felt that Sartre "gave too much place to conscious intent, not enough to the intuitive element in creation" and that he "hadn't really appreciated *Mythe de Sisyphe*" (279). The essay is, however, so central to any student's understanding of *The Stranger*, that a brief summary is offered.

Sartre begins by making a clear distinction between the two meanings which Camus gives to the word 'absurd': "the absurd is both a state of fact and the lucid awareness which certain people acquire of this state of fact" (Sartre 108). The "fact" is "nothing less than man's relation to the world ... [the unbridgeable gap] between man's drive towards the eternal and the *finite* character of his existence" (emphasis in original Sartre 109); it is "an inseparable part of the human condition" (Sartre 110). For Camus, "the tragedy of human existence lies in the absence of any transcendence" (Sartre 116).

Sartre next clarifies Camus' use of the word 'stranger' to describe Meursault by comparing him with "Somerset Maugham's savages before the arrival of the clergyman" and to Prince Mishkin in Dostoyevsky's *The Idiot* (Sartre 111). All are innocents for whom values (and therefore actions) have no meaning, and one choice is as good as another. For Meursault, "[a]ll that counts is the present and the concrete" (Sartre 113). He is "one of those terrible innocents who shock society by not accepting the rules of its game" (Sartre 111). Sartre insists that the novel aims only to present this character not to explain or to justify him or to prove any theory, "The Stranger is not an explanatory book" (Sartre 111). Whilst *Myth* explores the "idea" of the absurd, *The Stranger* gives the reader the "feeling

... plunges us without comment into the 'climate' of the absurd" (Sartre 114).

In considering Camus' technique, Sartre dismisses parallels with Kafka and finds comparisons with Hemmingway of limited value. He describes Camus' method in *The Stranger* as inserting "a glass partition between the reader and his characters" which is achieved by filtering all perceptions through the mind of the narrator, Meursault, a mind which "is so constructed as to be transparent to things and opaque to meanings" (Sartre 117), a mind which perceives life as nothing more or less than "a series of present moments" (Sartre 118). Sartre argues that this explains the sentence structures used in the narrative, "Each sentence is a present instant ... The world is destroyed and reborn from sentence to sentence ... The sentences in *The Stranger* are islands. We bounce from sentence to sentence, from void to void" (Sartre 119). Camus carefully conceals the causal links between incidents by using connectives like "'and,' 'but,' 'then,' and 'just then,' which evoke only disjunction, opposition, or mere addition" (Sartre 120). In substituting "the order of causality for chronological sequence" (Sartre 121), Camus achieves the result that, "All the sentences of his book are equal to each other, just as all the absurd man's experiences are equal" (Sartre 120).

Sartre's essay, remarkable as it is, tends to equate Camus and Meursault ignoring the artistic distance which the author maintains between himself and his protagonist. Sartre also underestimates the development of Meursault's character and of his understanding of the human condition. Although he mentions the final epiphany, it is not given the significance which it deserves.

Appendix 4: *The Stranger* (1967) directed by Luchino Visconti

French director Jean Renoir expressed an interest in making a film of *The Stranger* in 1949, but Camus' publisher Gallimard "demanded an exorbitant ten million francs for the screen rights, and the project died" (Todd 286). In 1967. seven years after Camus' death, Italian film director Luchino Visconti released *The Stranger* starring Marcello Mastroianni as Arthur Meursault and Anna Karina as Marie Cardona. The film was nominated for The Golden Lion, the highest prize given at the Venice Film Festival, but it was neither a critical nor a financial success on its release and has become one of the director's forgotten films whilst maintaining a cult following. Perhaps this failure is because this film is so different from Visconti's normal style, but I suspect that it has more to do with the essentially undramatic nature of Camus' novel. Visconti himself pointed to conflict between his own vision for the film which would have been based on selected scenes from the novel and that of Camus' widow, Francine, who rejected the first screenplay because it was not entirely faithful to the text. Visconti told *Le Monde*, "*The Stranger* became a fiasco because Albert Camus' widow demanded objective, absurd fidelity. In order to honor our contract I was forced to renounce the film I had always wanted to do and to confine myself strictly to the text" (quoted in Gay-Crosier 168).

The film begins after Meursault's arrest as he is being taken in handcuffs to his initial interrogation. The magistrate asks him if he has a lawyer, and Meursault replies that he does not think it is necessary because "I think my defense is quite simple." This is immediately followed by a flashback to Meursault running to catch the bus to Marengo. In this way, the film establishes Meursault as a commentator on the action of Part One of the novel with the expectation that his commentary will present Meursault's "simple" defense. The commentary is delivered in a series of voiceovers which stick pretty closely to the text of the novel. Thus the film's narrative perspective is very different from that of the novel where Meursault narrates from the beginning from the perspective of a condemned man following his final epiphany.

The film immediately establishes the heat and the oppressively bright light of the Algerian summer. Exterior shots are suffused with a bleaching white light, and sweat-marks are evident on clothing. An exception is the scene at the pool when Meursault meets Marie. Meursault comments that the day is "mild" and that "the sky filled my head with blue and gold." The scenes follow Part One of the novel quite faithfully, the most significant addition being a strain of eerie music which plays whenever Meursault feels under particular stress or when he feels uncomfortably dissociated from his surroundings. A sustained example is when Meursault and Marie are lying on the sand the Sunday they spend at Masoon's house. Marie is commenting on the Boss's offer of a move to Paris which Meursault has already rejected. Marie says, "I was thinking. Why not tell your boss that you have just reconsidered everything he said and accept that job in Paris next year. I'd come with you naturally. I'm dying to see Paris." The music shows that Meursault is sensing the pressure which their relationship is exerting to limit his freedom.

In depicting the three confrontations on the beach, the ominous music builds to a climax, and the bleaching white of the sun robs the scene of most of its color. As he returns to the beach alone, Meursault is shown to be suffering from the extreme heat; his shirt, saturated with sweat, clings to his back. The firing of the first shot is presented as an instinctive reaction to the reflection of the sun off of the Arab's knife; Meursault immediately looks shocked and disbelieving at what he has done. The remaining four shots are, however, clearly a separate and deliberate act. Meursault's commentary establishes that they are not the result of dissociation or confusion, "I shook off the veil of sweat and light that had blinded me." Rather, they are presented as deliberate acts designed to punish himself, "I realized that I had shattered the impassive stillness of the afternoon and the shimmering silence of the beach. And so I fired again." The paradoxical nature of the shots is that by an act of deliberate choice, Meursault places himself in a position where he will no longer have choice, "Four shots like four fateful raps on the door to my destiny."

As the action reaches the point at which the film began, no further rationale is given to explain Meursault as narrator; he simply continues to fulfill that role, though from what perspective it is not clear. The interrogation scenes establish the court officials as unsympathetic, even grotesque, characters who find Meursault both inexplicable and offensive. The magistrate appears almost demented when brandishing the crucifix in Meursault's face and demanding that he accept Christ's sacrifice.

The dialogue of the trial sticks very closely to the novel, but in presenting the trial in visual terms the emphasis on Meursault being tried for the way he lived his life (his failure to love his mother and to respond appropriately to her death, and his associating with the criminal Sintès) to the virtual exclusion of the actual shooting of the Arab becomes very clear. Not a single Arab is shown in the courtroom. The court officials are presented as grotesque and the court proceedings as anachronistic. The helpless frustration of Meursault as he hears himself discussed is clear, as is his inability to explain his action in firing the shots when he is given the opportunity to do so. The scene where the guilty verdict is given is particularly telling: the judges are wearing symbolic black and red robes which seem to be from a previous century, and the chief judge wears comic-looking *pince nez* to read the verdict in language which is ridiculously formal and official.

The director's problem with the concluding scenes in the jail is a more extreme version of the problems posed by filming the entire novel: *The Stranger* is the story of Meursault's intellectual growth. The drama is psychological, and as such it is virtually impossible to present Camus' meaning in terms of action. Visconti addresses this challenge in two ways. Firstly, Meursault's thoughts are presented in extended voiceovers, and secondly the important series of temptations through which Meursault passes are compressed in a short sequence of two minutes during which Meursault passes from being terrified that the guards will come for him to understanding that "it makes very little difference whether one dies at the age of thirty or at the age of seventy for once you're dead it doesn't matter how or when you died."

The climactic scene with the chaplain is, of course, more dramatic though their conflict is one of philosophy so their dialogue tends to be rather wordy. The chaplain comes across as a sympathetic character, but also a weak one: it is clear that, when he speaks of every person having doubts about their certainties, he is unconsciously speaking of his own fragile faith. Meursault's final epiphany is presented very powerfully in voiceover. He has no sooner understood that happiness is possible in life than the guards enter the cell, bind his hands behind his back, and take Meursault to execution.

Appendix 5: Guide to Further Reading

Olivier Todd's *Albert Camus: A Life* (1997) is a detailed and clear biography. The emphasis throughout is on Camus the man and the writer, largely leaving the reader to make connections between biography and the interpretation of individual works.

English Showalter's *The Stranger Humanity and the Absurd* equally satisfies the needs of the general reader and of the advanced student. It provides a clear reading of the novel taking a thematic (rather than chapter-by-chapter) approach.

Raymond Gay-Crosier's *The Stranger* comprehensively places the novel in its biographical, historical and cultural context. The chapter analyzing the novel stresses the "inescapable ambiguity" of the text rather than offering one reading (95). The review of the critical responses to the novel since its publication will interest the advanced student.

Catherine Brosman's *Albert Camus* also comprehensively places Camus' works in their biographical, historical and cultural context. The more general scope of the book allows relatively little space for analysis of *The Stranger* itself.

Patrick McCarthy's *Camus The Stranger: A Student Guide* (2004) uses the original French text with McCarthy's translation. The book places the novel in the context of Camus' life and of his cultural, political, and philosophical background and evaluates it using a range of critical approaches appropriate to the advanced student. McCarthy's central thesis is that, because of the incongruity between Part One and Part Two, the novel "resists interpretation" (79).

Harold Bloom's *Albert Camus's The Stranger* (2008) contains a 'Summary and Analysis' section which is rather more summary than analysis. The book also gives ten selected critical readings which are much more useful though rather short.

Bibliography

Bespaloff, Rachel. "The World of the Man Condemned to Die." Brée 92-107. Print.

Bloom, Harold, ed. *Albert Camus's The Stranger*. 1st ed. New York: Infobase Publishing, 2008. Print.

Bloom, Harold. *Novelists and Novels*. 1st ed. Philadelphia Chelsea House, 2005. Print.

Bloom, Ryan. "Lost in Translation: What the First Line of 'The Stranger' Should Be." *New Yorker Online*. 15 May 2012: n. page. Web. 18 Jun. 2012.

Brosman, Catherine. *Literary Masters Volume 8 Albert Camus*. 1st ed. Detroit: The Gale Group, 2001. Print.

Brée, Germaine. *Albert Camus*. 1st ed. New York: Columbia University Press, 1964. Print.

Brée, Germaine, ed. *Camus: A Collection of Critical Essays*. 1st ed. Englewood Cliffs: Prentice-Hall, 1962. Print.

Byrne, Rhonda. *The Secret*. 1st ed. New York: Simon & Schuster, 2006. Print.

Camus, Albert. *A Happy Death*. Trans. Richard Howard. 1st Vintage International Ed. New York: Random House, 1995. Print.

---. *The Myth of Sisyphus and Other Essays*. Trans. Justin O'Brien. 1st Vintage International Ed. New York: Random House, 1991. Print.

---. *The Stranger*. Trans. Matthew Ward. 1st Vintage International Ed. New York: Random House, 1989. Print.

Champigny, Robert. "Ethics and Aesthetics in *The Stranger*." Brée 122-131. Print.

Doubrovsky, Serge. "The Ethics of Albert Camus." Brée 71-84. Print.

Delahoyde, Michael. "Camus, *The Stranger*." *20th Century Arts & Humanities*. Washington State University, 2005. Web. 18 Jun 2012.

Edwards , Jonathan and Smolinski, Reiner , Editor. "Sinners in the Hands of an Angry God. A Sermon Preached at Enfield, July 8th, 1741." *Electronic Texts in American Studies*. University of Nebraska - Lincoln, Web. 13 Sep.

Gay-Crosier, Raymond. *Literary Masterpieces Volume 8 The Stranger*. 1st ed. Detroit: The Gale Group, 2002. Print.

Lottman, Herbert. *Albert Camus A Biography*. 1st ed. New York: Doubleday and Company, 1979. Print.

John, S. Beynon. "Albert Camus: A British View." Brée 85-91. Print.

McCarthy, Patrick. *Camus The Stranger: A Student Guide*. 2nd ed. New York: Cambridge University Press, 2004. Print.

Rhein, Phillip. *Albert Camus*. 1st ed. Twayne Publishers, 1969. Print.

Sartre, Jean-Paul. "An Explication of *The Stranger*." Brée 108-121. Print.

Scherr, Arthur. "Camus's *The Stranger*." *Explicator* 59.3 Spring 2001: 149-53. Print.

Showalter Jr., English. *The Stranger Humanity and the Absurd*. 1st ed. Boston: Twayne Publishers, 1989. Print.

Simpson, David. "Albert Camus (1913—1960)." *The Internet Encyclopedia of Philosophy (IEP)*. 2005. Web. 13 Jul 2012.

SparkNotes Editors. "SparkNote on *The Stranger*." SparkNotes.com. SparkNotes LLC. 2003. Web. 8 Jun. 2012.

Sprintzen, Adrian, and David van den Hoven. *Sartre and Camus: A Historical Confrontation*. 1st ed. Amherst: Humanity Books, 2004. Print.

Todd, Olivier. *Albert Camus: A Life*. 1st ed. New York: Carroll & Graf Publishers, 1997.Print.

Visconti, Luchino. *The Stranger*. Film. 23 Feb 2009. YouTube. 2 Aug 2012.

Zaretsky, Robert. *Albert Camus: Elements of a Life*. 1st ed. New York, USA: Cornell University Press, 2010. 1-160. Print.

About the Author

Ray Moore was born in Nottingham, England in 1950. He obtained his Master's Degree in Literature at Lancaster University in 1974 and then taught in secondary education for twenty-eight years before relocating to Florida with his wife in 2002. There he taught English and Information Technology in the International Baccalaureate program at Vanguard High School in Ocala.

He is now a full-time writer and fitness fanatic.

Also by Ray Moore

Fiction:

Investigations of The Reverend Lyle Thorne (published October 2012)

Further Investigations of The Reverend Lyle Thorne (published March 2013)

Non-fiction:

"The General Prologue" by Geoffrey Chaucer: A Critical Introduction (published January 2013)

Contact Information:

Email: moore.ray1@yahoo.com

CPSIA information can be obtained at www.ICGtesting.com
Printed in the USA
LVOW071442231212

312975LV00002B/196/P